NAUGHTY GIRL'S
Guide to
LOS ANGELES

FOR REVIEW ONLY
SMITH PUBLICITY, INC.
856-489-8654

Naughty Girl's Guide to Los Angeles
www.NaughtyTravelGirl.com

Published by Naughty Girl Press
1158 26th St. Suite 207
Santa Monica, CA 90403
www.NaughtyGirlPress.com

Text © 2012 Sienna Sinclaire
Photography © 2012 Sienna Sinclaire except where noted on page 391

First Edition 2012

ISBN 978-0-9852123-0-8

All rights reserved under international and Pan-American copyright conventions. No part of this publication may be reproduced, stored in a retrieval system or transmitted in any form or by any means, electronic, mechanical, photocopying, recording, or otherwise, without prior written permission of the copyright owner.

Every effort was made to make sure that this book is as up-to-date as possible at the time of going to press. Some details such as websites, telephone numbers and addresses are likely to change. And some places may even go out of business by the time you read this book. My advice would be to call or visit the businesses websites before visiting. The author and publisher of *Naughty Girl's Guide to Los Angeles* cannot accept responsibility for facts that have become outdated or situations that arise from the use of this book.

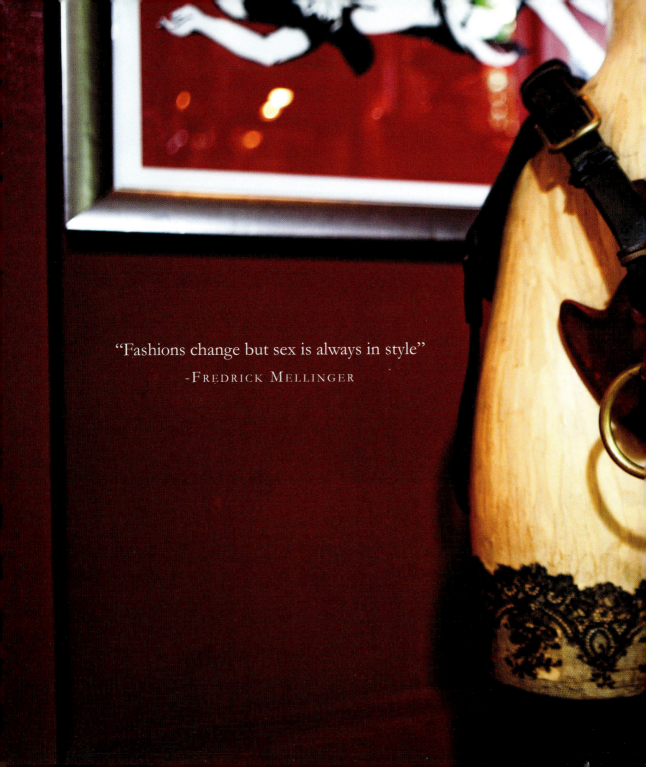

"Fashions change but sex is always in style"
-Fredrick Mellinger

To my naughty travel companion.

Contents

Who is the Naughty Girl? 13

NAUGHTY HISTORY 15
Los Angeles' Naughty History 17
Sex in Books 41
Sex in Videos 45
Sex in Films 49

NAUGHTY TRAVEL 53
Planning Your Trip 55
What To Pack 57
Secret Rendezvous 65
   Solo Getaway 67
   Girl's Getaway 71
   Lover's Getaway 73
   Kinky Getaway 77
Best Places For a Secret Rendezvous 81
Finding A Date 84
Motel Fetish 89
Naughty Tip #1: Motel Rendezvous 95

NAUGHTY BY DAY 99
Naughty Day Tours 101
   Things To See 102

  Places To Visit 106
  Naughty Home Tour 117
Sexy Tours 121
Naughty Events 125
  Adult Industry Events 130
  Fetish Events 131
Sex Ed Classes 135
  Naughty Classes 136
  Fetish Classes 142
Sexy Dance Classes 145
  Pole Dancing & Striptease Classes 146
  Burlesque Classes 152
  Belly Dance Classes 154
  Salsa Classes 161
  Tahitian and Hula Dancing 164
  Other Sexy Classes 166
Sexy Fitness 171
Host a Naughty Party 173
Nude Beaches 183

NAUGHTY SHOPPING 189
Beauty 191
History of Lingerie in Los Angeles 197
  High-end Lingerie 200
  Lingerie Stores 207
Sex & Spikes 211
  Lingerie Shoe Stores 214

High-end Shoe Designers 217
Vintage Shoe Stores 220
Department Shoe Stores 221
History of Dildos in Los Angeles.. 223
Sex Toy Stores 225
Burlesque & Pinup Stores 229
Fetish Stores 235
Naughty Treats 243
Erotic Art 247

NAUGHTY BY NIGHT 251
Swinging in L.A. 253
Where to Swing 257
Naughty Tip #2: How To Swing 261
L.A. After Dark 265
L.A.'s Sexiest Restaurants 266
Naughty Themed Dinners 275
L.A.'s Sexiest Bars 277
Sexy L.A. Singers 286
L.A.'s Sexiest Clubs 288
L.A.'s Sexy Nightlife 295
Naughty Parties 295
Salsa Clubs 297
Sexy Dancers 299
Flamenco Shows 300
Belly Dancing Shows 301
Fetish Clubs 304

    Fetish Playrooms 308
  Naughty Tip #3: Fetish Play...311
  A Brief History of Burlesque in L.A. 315
    Burlesque Performers 319
    Burlesque Shows 324
  L.A. Strip Clubs 327
  Halloween in L.A. 335

NAUGHTY BUSINESS 339
  Erotic Talk Radio Shows 341
  Erotic News 345
  Erotic Photographers...349
  How To Get Started in the Adult Business 355
  Porn Star Biographies 361
  Adult Industry Books 367
  Adult Industry Services 371
  Adult Modeling 375

Three Ways to Take L.A. Home With You 379
About The Author 383
About The Photographer 384
Bibliography 385
Index 387
Photo Credits 391

WHO IS THE NAUGHTY GIRL?

All of us ladies have an inner "Naughty Girl." Sometimes we just need a little extra help to bring her out. This book was written for anyone who wants to release their inner Naughty Girl. I'm here to show you how to do it while keeping your clothes on. It's not difficult at all. Bringing your Naughty Girl to life, even for a little while, can be quite liberating and give you a new sense of freedom, delight and power.

Whether you live in L.A. or you're just visiting, this book will help you explore another side to L.A.—its naughty side. Sex and beauty are openly worshipped here, yet so much of its naughty side remains in the shadows. You just need to know where to look. Even if you don't live in L.A. or never plan to visit you can still learn all about its racy history.

My hope is that after you read this book you'll be intrigued to discover the steamy, sexy side of Los Angeles while exploring your secret desires. It'll be a fun adventure, and I'm delighted to be your kinky tour guide.

x o x o   *Sienna Sinclaire*

Naughty History

L.A.'S NAUGHTY HISTORY

Los Angeles has a long history of being naughty—a tradition that hasn't let up one bit over the years. L.A. was voted both the "World's Sluttiest" and "Sexiest" city in 2005 by GridSkipper.com. Los Angeles, the birthplace of the casting couch and celebrity sex scandals, is home to the world's porn industry. It's also the biggest distributor of dildos and vibrators in the world and where Hugh Hefner and Larry Flynt run their porn empires.

Los Angeles was the original "Sin City" long before Las Vegas. It was (and still is, in some ways) the city that parents warned their kids about during the beginning of the film industry. Many of those who came from small towns and the heartland to L.A. to seek fame, fortune and a better life were easily sucked into the sins that a big city had to offer. People still flock here every year with hopes of making it on the big screen. The only difference now is that everyone can make it big in L.A. and be on film if they're willing to accept porn as an option.

THE RISE OF HOLLYWOOD

The first movie ever to be filmed in Hollywood, *In Old California*, was directed by D.W. Griffith in early 1910. He came from New York City to California in search of better weather (New York's freezing winters and scorching summers would delay movie shoots) and to avoid the high filming fees charged in NYC. After his success, other film directors flocked en masse to Hollywood to set up studios and begin filming so they could take advantage of California's perfect weather, ample land, varied scenery and cheap labor. Thus began the rise of Hollywood.

THE JAZZ AGE: THE DECADE OF SEX

Sex was everywhere in the 1920s. It was in advertising and early cinema (although nowhere near as prevalent as it is now). It was in art. It was on the radio, it was in roadside motels and it was in the back seats of cars. The 1920s shaped the ideal of the female body and how it would be displayed to the world. That image endures even today. The Jazz Age had a huge influence on Hollywood and, by extension, the rest of the world.

Hollywood had a young population, making it a haven for sexual experimentation. Young fans weren't just watching the Hollywood films, they were imitating what they saw on screen. For many this was the first time they saw scantily dressed women, people kissing, women speaking dialogue laced with double entendres and couples acting out love scenes on screen. Movies weren't just for entertainment. They taught male viewers how to kiss a woman on areas of her body other than just her lips, and taught female viewers how to boost their sex appeal by dressing and looking like Hollywood starlets.

The 1910s and 1920s were decades of experimentation and "free love" long before the 1970s. The early 1900s were the first time in Western history that women were making enough money to live on their own and realize that having money meant freedom. Women weren't sitting around at home anymore waiting for male callers—they were out on their own meeting gentlemen friends at bars, restaurants or dance halls. Women were calling the shots and men were taking notice as Flapper girls were hiking up their skirts, gyrating to the Charleston, boozing, staying up till dawn and necking and more in the back seat of cars. Unfortunately, this newfound sexual freedom and expression didn't last long as the Depression hit Americans hard and the Will Hays Codes banished racy content on the silver screen. Just as we were starting to come out of the uptight Victorian Era, the Will Hays Code brought us back into it. It would be an additional forty years before we had another sexual revolution (which, sadly, would again be short-lived with the rise of AIDS in the 1980s).

SEX IN CINEMA

Movie makers started advertising L.A. to the world as soon as they began shooting their first films in Hollywood. They made it known that Los Angeles was the place where the young came to live and play—and to indulge in forbidden delights.

Pre-Code Hollywood films were full of sexual imagery and innuendo. Hollywood was constantly pushing the limits of on-screen sex. They devoted entire movies to cheating wives, dancing flappers, boozing women and seducing mistresses. Fans couldn't get enough of these "explicit" films. For many, this was the first time they saw a woman in lingerie and for others these movies were educational in that they gave cues to people how to date and interact with the opposite sex. People flocked to movie theatres, but the decadent party of the past two decades was about to come to an end. Many would be feeling a hangover for decades to come.

WILL HAYS-CODE: THE PARTY'S OVER

Hollywood cinema changed in July 1934. During that month, the Production Code Administration, popularly known as the Wills Hays Code, began to mercilessly regulate the content of Hollywood motion pictures. For the next thirty years, cinematic space was a patrolled landscape with secure

NAUGHTY HISTORY

perimeters and well-defined borders. Adopted under duress at the urging of priests and politicians, Hollywood's in-house policy of self-censorship set the boundaries for what could be seen, heard and implied on screen.

In pre-Code Hollywood films, sometimes what was suggested and what the spectator didn't see was often more naughty than what was portrayed on screen. Under the Code, an image not even depicted on screen but merely planted in the spectator's mind would be too arousing and thus banned to the cutting room floor. The Code devoted considerable attention to expunging sex from films. It promulgated the conservative view that any relaxation of traditional sexual morals would precipitate a loosening of marital bonds. Non-marital sex was not only wrong in and of itself, it also threatened the institution of marriage. Thus, the main objective with the ban on sex was to maintain the sanctity of marriage and the home.

The Code wasn't just limited to what was on screen, it also crept into advertisements for films. In December 1933, the Wills Hays Code created a list of commandments that not only prohibited certain advertisements, but also revealed the popularity of sex in media at the time.

Variety magazine published the entire contents of the code on February 19, 1930, but these are just the ones for images and text in advertising:

- "Thou shalt not photograph kissing, necking or any type of lovemaking scenes in which the principals are in a horizontal position. In any kissing scene the pose must be standing, or sitting.

- Thou shalt not photograph girls in scenes in which the femmes pull up their skirts to show a lengthy display of legs and the unfastening of a garter.

- Thou shalt not use the word "courtesan" or words meaning the same in any advertising copy used for the exploitation of pictures."

The Wills Hays Code worried that images and written words in advertisements would lure audiences to movie theatres where they might imitate what they saw on screen. The big film studios voluntarily cleaned up their act, adopted the Hays Motion Picture Production Code and banished sexual themes and imagery from the silver screen. Many brave filmmakers challenged the Code over the next thirty years. One example is the movie *Outlaw*, in which Howard Hughes had a special bra made to push up and highlight the wonderful cleavage of Jane Russell.

NAUGHTY STARLETS

Movies and their sexy stars brought celebrity scandals. People couldn't get enough of any published sex gossip they could find on the bedroom activities of their favorite stars (and they still can't today). Fans wanted to know all about their favorite Hollywood starlets. For their part, the actresses never seemed to let them down with scandalous stories. Even with the Will Hays Code in effect, Hollywood starlets were still pushing the limits of sex on and off screen.

Many starlets were more than happy to pose nude (Jean Harlow, Barbara LaMarr, Hedy Lamarr, Jayne Mansfield and Marilyn Monroe were just a few) and sleep their way to the top via the casting couch. Everyone in Hollywood seemed to be sleeping with everyone else as Maximillien De Lafayette pointed out in his book *Hollywood Earth Shattering Scandals: The Infamous Villains, Nymphomaniacs and Shady Characters in Motion Pictures*. He states that Marilyn Monroe could list Frank Sinatra, Marlon Brando, Clark Cable, Humphrey Bogart and John F. Kennedy as lovers, to name just a few. And that Kennedy was quite the man in Hollywood—he was said to have slept with over twenty starlets apart from Marilyn Monroe. Another stallion in Hollywood that De Lafayette mentions was Gary Cooper, who slept with some of the most famous actresses, including Grace Kelly, Clara Bow, Marlene Dietrich, Barbara Payton, Rita Hayworth, Veronica Lake, Barbara Stanwyck, Joan Crawford and Louise Brooks. Cooper's list of conquests is too long to list. As you can tell, everyone was getting it on in Hollywood.

The life of a Hollywood actress wasn't always glamorous. Barbara Payton, a gorgeous blonde starlet, became a rising star in the early 1950s and was making $10,000 a week. However, her drug and alcohol abuse ended her movie career. She became so desperate for money that she eventually became a street prostitute in L.A.'s Skid Row and died of heart and liver failure in San Diego at her parents' home.

Then there were those Hollywood starlets who lost their movie careers due to the Will Hays Code. Mae West is probably the best-known case. Her sex appeal and innuendos are what made her big in Hollywood in the early years. Now that she couldn't show off her well-known assets or imply anything sexual on screen, she lost her appeal to movie studios. After the Wills Hays Code went into effect, sex kittens like Mae West moved to the side to make room for a new Hollywood starlet in town—Shirley Temple. Hollywood was cleaning up and Shirley Temple was their solution.

HOLLYWOOD TRYSTS: CHATEAU MARMONT

Hollywood actors and actresses had many places in L.A. to get frisky, but the most famous was the Chateau Marmont. In 1939 Harry Cohn, founder of Columbia Pictures, described it best when he said, "If you must get in trouble, do it at the Chateau Marmont." And do it they did!

Built in 1927, the Chateau Marmont opened in February 1929 as an apartment house. However, due to the Depression not everyone could afford the high rent and it was quickly turned into a hotel. Ever since then the Chateau Marmont has been a naughty playground for celebrities and high-end call girls.

You can be yourself or whomever you want while staying at this exclusive hotel. Don't be surprised if the Chateau Marmont brings out a mischievous side of you that you've never seen before, as it's known to turn even the chastest person into the naughtiest sex kitten. With its secretive staff, private entry and elevator that whisk you straight to your room without anyone noticing, this hotel was designed for naughty romps. Plus, its sexy vintage rooms and secluded bungalows have kitchens, so you never have to leave your naughty oasis.

FREDERICK'S OF HOLLYWOOD:
NAUGHTY LINGERIE COMES TO L.A.

Frederick Mellinger is probably responsible for turning more housewives into sexual powerhouses than most people realize. Mellinger thought up his lingerie business after asking his WWII buddies what scantily clothing they liked women to wear and decided to create a women's lingerie line from a man's point of view. He moved to Hollywood in 1946 and opened his well-known lingerie shop, Frederick's of Hollywood.

He was well-known and loved by movie stars who went to him for his sexy, provocative European-style lingerie. Hollywood directors went to him for custom designs for their movies. But it wasn't until the 1960s that his business really took off when he opened his stores in malls around the country and was embraced by housewives from suburbia to the Bible belt. Women flocked to his stores and purchased from his catalogs in hopes of looking like their favorite Hollywood starlet. And many husbands were more than happy to foot the bill for their wife's extravagances.

As Mellinger loved to say, "Fashions change but sex is always in style." Hollywood, of course, lived and died by this motto.

BURLESQUE

Sexy fashions from Frederick's of Hollywood soon began showing up on women who were paid to take off those sexy clothes. Burlesque dancers filled their closets with sexy lingerie and the burlesque movement surged in 1940s Hollywood. Many wonderful burlesque venues—the Follies, the Burbank Theater, the Florentine Gardens and Ciro's—opened during this time and were often packed with businessmen, artists, musicians, movie producers and undercover cops.

Hollywood paid attention. Soon famous dancers like Lili St. Cyr, Tempest Storm and Betty Rowland were appearing in movies to draw in male viewers who lived outside California and couldn't get to these burlesque clubs. Dance routines in movies took moves from burlesque acts and soon had famous actresses doing everything but stripping down to pasties. The Hays Code, of course, tried to keep burlesque out of films. As a result, many underground burlesque films like *Striporama* were produced. They were shown mostly late nights and at stag parties across the nation.

NEW HOLLYWOOD:
THE WILLS HAYS CODE COMES TO AN END

It wasn't until the late 1940s that cracks began to appear in the structure of the Wills Hays Code with the films *Johnny Belinda* (1948) and *Pinky* (1949). Between the late 1940s and early 1950s parts of the Code were being changed to allow taboo subjects such as rape, miscegenation, adultery, prostitution and abortion in films.

By the late 1950s, people were seeking sexual excitement and escapism in film, so movies got naughtier and cheekier as the "Ozzie and Harriet" 1950s began to roll into the "free love" 1960s. Films like *Suddenly Last Summer* (1959) and *Some Like It Hot* (1959) were released without a certificate of approval from the MPAA (although Billy Wilder did make some cuts to *Some Like It Hot*) and were box office hits. The Wills Hays Code began to crack under popular opinion and the weight of money the studios were earning on films helped push the boundaries of censorship.

The 1960s began a return to subject matter not seen in films since the early 1930s. The MPAA couldn't ignore the popularity or quality of some of these movies and had to grant approval of them. Granted, many directors still cut certain scenes or dialogue, but more and more directors were pushing the boundaries. By the mid-1960s many directors couldn't care less about the Code and were making the films they wanted. *Who's Afraid of Virginia Woolf?* was released in 1966 and was nominated for Best Picture even though it had explicit language. The MPAA approved it—despite the language—and soon enforcement of the Code became impossible.

The Code edifice finally came crumbling down on November 1, 1968 when the motion picture industry adopted the more favorable (although highly subjective) MPAA film rating system. The ratings were *G*, *M*, *R* and *X*. *M* was changed to *GP* in 1970 and then to *PG* in 1972. *PG-13* was created in 1984 when parents and other viewers complained about the violence in *PG* movies like *Gremlins* and the *Indiana Jones* movies. In 1990, the *X* rating was replaced by *NC-17*. The MPAA hadn't trademarked the *X* rating and it had been adopted by the porn industry. Many movie studios complained that an *X* rating would doom their film because it would be branded as porn by the general public, so the

NC-17 rating was reluctantly accepted by the studios (although studios still strive to avoid it when possible).

Hollywood's "golden age" began with the Wills Hays Code and ended with its demise.

PORNO CHIC: THE GOLDEN AGE OF PORN

The Golden Age of porn began with the surprising, massive success of *Deep Throat* (1972) and the subsequent success of *Behind the Green Door*. *Deep Throat* was made for pocket change (from a Hollywood studio perspective) and brought in millions. It's still one of most successful theatrical releases of all time. These films built a cult audience that began in grindhouse theatres and spread out to movie houses in the Midwest. It became fashionable for men and women to watch and discuss such films as *The Devil in Miss Jones* and *Score*.

Porn stars became household names. Linda Lovelace, Marilyn Chambers, Annie Sprinkle, Seka, Harry Reems, Ron Jeremy and John Holmes (a.k.a. "Johnny Wadd") were as well-known as baseball players, news anchors and the stars of Oscar-winning films. Marilyn Chambers eventually worked in mainstream movies, being one of the first crossover porn actors.

L.A. movie theatres started showing popular porn films to boost their

revenue and meet customer demand. The same couples coming in to see *The French Connection* were returning for the late show of *Debbie Does Dallas*. Stud's was the most popular adult movie theatre in town and still stands today—although it's now a gay theatre.

Linda Lovelace, the star of *Deep Throat*, believed that the porn industry would eventual merge with the mainstream film industry. She was right. The porn industry has a huge influence on mainstream media even to the point of helping VHS become the prominent video media over Betamax in the 1980s and high-definition winning over Blu-Ray in the millennium.

NUDIE MAGAZINES

Films weren't the only medium reinterpreting how Americans' sex lives should be portrayed. *Playboy* became the most popular magazine among men (and probably among many curious housewives), with none other than Marilyn Monroe being on the cover and in the centerfold of the first issue!

Hugh "Hef" Hefner moved to L.A. in 1971 to run his publishing empire, where he flaunted his lavish lifestyle. The Playboy Mansion became the spot to be seen in L.A. The parties there were, and still are, legendary. Rock stars, famous artists, best-selling authors, Hollywood glitterati, and, of course, stunning women could be found there on any given day or night. It's still known for wild parties, reality TV and lovely ladies.

Larry Flynt, publisher of *Hustler*, made his fortune in the Midwest with his strip clubs and a nationally distributed magazine. His porn empire soon outgrew conservative Ohio and he eventually moved to L.A. He bought the adult film company VCA Pictures in 2003, and now Larry Flynt Productions is one of the top-selling porn studios in the world (especially with its porn parody films). He also opened the Hustler store and Hustler Casino. In many ways, he's more powerful than Hugh Hefner and has brought a naughtier "girl next door" to the masses with his publications.

THE '80S: CHANGES IN SEXUAL ATTITUDES

An unstoppable force burst into homes in the 1980s. It would change the porn and mainstream movie industries forever. Movie theatres would tremble at the sight and mention of it. What was it? None other than the VCR.

The video cassette recorder allowed everyone to watch porn in the privacy of their homes—finally. Mail-order porn became an overnight success and video stores clamored to open an "adults only" section to meet demand. Adult movie stores popped up on almost every corner. They mainly catered to men and soon took on a "seedy" feel that wasn't popular among women. The porn industry, formerly confined to grindhouse theatres, flourished. The industry pushed for the cheaper VHS format over the better-quality (but more expensive) Betamax format so they could put out more material at a faster rate to meet all the demand. Movie theatres felt the end was near. Many porn theatres closed their doors for good while mainstream theatres held on for dear life.

Just when the porn industry was at the height of its home-video success, the Center for Disease Control and Prevention (also known as the CDC) published a report on June 4, 1981, about five homosexual men in L.A. who had contracted a rare form of pneumonia. AIDS crept into Hollywood and began decimating adult movie studios. John Holmes was the best-known casualty and the "free love" attitude left over from the 1970s porn industry disappeared. Sexual expression went back underground again since people were scared of this new disease and had no idea what it was or how it spread.

BURLESQUE REVIVAL

As the 1980s faded as fast as a post-orgasm cigarette, in the 1990s many dancers in L.A. realized that people were hungry for titillation. The "New Burlesque" movement was formed and soon exotic dancers and sexy costumes were brought back to the masses. L.A.'s Velvet Hammer troupe led the charge and caused a revival that has now spread across the country.

AIDS wasn't forgotten, but the American public was more educated about it now and was again ready to express their desires. Most people were happy with just the tease and the "New Burlesque" movement gave it to them and encouraged women to embrace their naughty side. Even strip clubs saw resurgence in popularity. And today there are so many pole-dance and "strip-fitness" classes available that it's almost impossible to keep count of the ones just in L.A.

SEX SELLS: THE HOLLYWOOD MADAM

While most twenty-two-year-old gals were attending college, auditioning for film or working as a waitress (or all of the above), Heidi Fleiss was managing a prostitution ring. She claimed to have made her first million dollars in just four months. She was the most successful madam in early 1990s Hollywood and had many famous and wealthy clients (which she has never named).

Her success as a madam ended in 1993 when she was arrested for multiple charges, supposedly after envious pimps and madams worked their connections with local police to put the heat on her. Federal and state charges were filed in 1994, but her state conviction was overturned in 1996. Her federal trial began that year and she was convicted of tax evasion and sentenced to seven years in prison. She was released to a halfway house two months later and had to perform 370 hours of community service. She was released in September 1999 after serving three years.

WOMEN OF PORN

Porn may still be a man's world, but women are taking it over one sex scene at a time. Ever since the early days of porn, women were little more than eye candy used to sell movies, magazines and other sex products to men. Today, however, female performers are taking charge of their careers by producing their own films, opening couples-friendly sex stores, launching adult websites, publishing pornographic magazines and writing thoughtful, analytical sex commentary.

For instance, the smoking-hot duo of Juli Ashton and Tiffany Granath helped launch Playboy Radio and came up with the concept for "Nightcalls Radio." Holly Randall followed in her mother Suze's footsteps and has become an erotic photographer, shooting some of the most beautiful women in porn. Theresa Flynt helped restructure the Hustler empire and now runs the Hustler stores. Jessica Drake not only stars in porn films but also directs, hosts her own radio show on Playboy Radio and has her own charity. Nina Hartley is famous for pioneering hardcore how-to videos and has become a well-known and well-respected author on sexuality.

HOLLYWOOD OF TODAY

Not much has changed since the early days of Hollywood. There have always been sex scandals. However, the Internet has brought out more of them and at a much faster rate than even ten years ago. Social networking sites and video uploading allow people to post whatever they want and in a blink of an eye. Nothing makes a great story like a Hollywood sex scandal—and we have plenty of them.

Let's face it, Hollywood and the greater L.A. area wouldn't be as interesting without sex scandals. There are those who make headlines with their sex scandals (Sandra Bullock's husband Jesse James) and there are those in the shadows who only make a minor splash if they end up sleeping with Charlie Sheen (Bree Olsen).

How much would we really know about Paris Hilton, Pamela Anderson or Kim Kardashian without their sex scandals? Their "accidentally leaked" scandals only served to boost their careers. Kim Kardashian is the perfect example because now she is everywhere (and I mean everywhere!). Even becoming famous or being a celebrity has changed drastically since the beginnings of Hollywood.

Charlie Sheen has been dating escorts and porn stars (such as Ginger Lynn at the outset) for years. It's only recently that his bedroom parties have

NAUGHTY HISTORY

been brought to light in mainstream media. He makes no bones about what he does or with whom he sleeps. He thinks he's "winning," and in many ways he is. His sex life enhanced his reputation with the media and the studios, which paid him millions before his last meltdown.

Charlie Sheen would have no trouble finding high-end escorts because there are tons of them in L.A. They can be found online and usually start at $2,000 for only a few hours of fun. If you're looking for a full night of fun then expect to pay up to $10,000 (or more, depending on the hours). You never know when you'll be out at dinner and see a gentleman with his lady friend or when you'll see one walking through the lobby of a high-end hotel carrying a discreet bag. High-end escorts not only work solo, some also work for escorting agencies that can provide ladies for celebrity parties, Playboy Mansion events or a night of fun at Charlie Sheen's house. High-end escorts make very good money and many live a lavish L.A. life.

L.A. is the porn capital of the world. There are just as many, if not more, porn stars living in L.A. than models living in NYC. They're in line with you at the grocery store, asking you for the cream at Starbucks or sitting next to you at your favorite bar. People visit L.A. in hopes of running into their favorite celebrity, but nowadays you're more likely to run into a porn star or escort and not even know it.

HOLLYWOOD OF TOMORROW

Los Angeles, to say the least, has been a wild mixture of sun, sand, sex, scandals and sensations since the beginning of Hollywood. You can find anything you want here, which you're about to find out in this book. Many people flocked here to pursue dreams and still do. However, many find other dreams they didn't realize they had—such as getting into porn. You can find a lot of hidden desires here. The town oozes sex and glamour. It can't be ignored, as it's on every billboard, in every shop window, on every movie screen and in every magazine publication. L.A. can be a rather provocative town. It's the perfect place to let down your hair and embrace your inner naughty girl.

NAUGHTY HISTORY

PRIVATE

THE BEST OF THE REVOLUTIONARY SWEDISH SEX MAGAZINE

Inside this 5-Volume, 960-page boxed set:

44 Gorgeous PRIVATE Girls in 800 Stunning Pictures

Printed from the Original Color Transparencies Including Outtakes & Never-Before-Seen Photos

Vintage ART, ADS and EDITORIALS Complete this Fascinating Look at the Birth of Pornography and the Infamous SWEDISH SIN

PRIVATE 1980 – 1989

PRIVATE
1980–1989

TASCHEN

seduced art & sex from antiquity to now MERRELL

TY THINGS LIZ GOLDWYN REGAN

SEX IN BOOKS

If you're flying or taking the train or even in the passenger seat on a road trip to L.A., you're going to need a good book. Since you're coming to L.A. for a naughty trip, you might as well start on the right foot with reading up on the naughty history of L.A., the porn industry and Hollywood's love of glamour and sex. Check out any of the following books for a good primer on the naughty side of L.A. and its scandalous history.

THE OTHER HOLLYWOOD: THE UNCENSORED ORAL HISTORY OF THE PORN FILM INDUSTRY
BY LEGS MCNEIL & JENNIFER OSBORNE

In this book you'll learn the "real" side of Hollywood. It's a world way naughtier than anyone could ever imagine. This is a history about the birth of the adult industry as told by the stars, filmmakers and other industry players who lived it. McNeil holds nothing back and publishes his interviews with no censoring. Everything is laid bare here, from the breakthrough of *Deep Throat* to the AIDS epidemic that devastated the porn industry in the '80s and '90s. Want to know the story behind Savannah's suicide or the Traci Lords scandal? Read about it in interviews from the people who were there.

PRE-CODE HOLLYWOOD: SEX, IMMORALITY, AND INSURRECTION IN AMERICAN CINEMA 1930-34
BY THOMAS DOHERTY

Ever wonder what movies were like before there were ratings? They were chock-full of sex, violence, drugs and booze. Pre-Code Hollywood films were considered too naughty for their time; therefore, all movies filmed during the Wills Hays Code Era were censored. Learn in detail the birth of Hollywood and how sex and immorality changed the way we watch films today. Also, learn how the new rating systems implemented in 1968 divided porn and Hollywood films into separate categories. This excellent book has the skinny on the cinematic lost gems you've likely never seen or even heard of.

EROTIC CINEMA
BY DOUGLAS KEESEY AND PAUL DUNCAN

Learn about Hollywood's naughty movie stars through the years. This book's erotic, picturesque journey of Hollywood films features femme fatales, homosexuality, sodomy, orgies, voyeurism and fanciful fetishes. What more could one ask for? It covers a wide swath of on-screen erotica and highlights ten of the sexiest films ever made—from *Last Tango in Paris* to *Y Tu Mama Tambien*.

HOLLYWOOD EARTH SHATTERING SCANDALS: THE INFAMOUS VILLAINS, NYMPHOMANIACS AND SHADY CHARACTERS IN MOTION PICTURES
BY MAXIMILLIEN DE LAFAYETTE

Take a deep look inside Hollywood's most famous movie stars' sex lives. Some stories are so shocking that they may change the way you think of some of your favorite movie stars. Many photos were never seen until this book was published because the photos were too naughty for the news at the time. The scandalous sex stories of many stars make the porn industry seem tame. There are many editions of this book; some are split into multiple parts. You can see mug shots, read about murder scandals, find out who let their Naughty Girl out on a regular basis and learn the names of all the women JFK took for a roll in the hay—and much, much more. No scandal is left untouched—be it from the classic or modern era of Hollywood.

SEX IN VIDEOS

Here are some movies to watch so that you can learn more about Hollywood's madams, the porn industry, pre-Code Hollywood films, the Playboy Mansion and the many models who pose nude—from webcam girls to traditional print models. These are the people who make Los Angeles "so L.A."

CALL ME: THE RISE AND FALL OF HEIDI FLEISS (2004) This little-seen TV movie premiered on the USA Network and stars Jamie-Lynn Sigler (best known as Meadow Soprano from *The Sopranos*) as Heidi Fleiss. She's super sexy in the role and, for a USA Network TV movie, this fairly risqué film includes scenes of sex and drug use. If you want to see what it's like to hire a high-priced call girl in L.A., or what your favorite movie stars did for fun with madam Fleiss's girls, this is the movie for you.

RATED X: A JOURNEY THROUGH PORN (1999) A good documentary for those who are curious about the adult industry. Director Dag Yngvesson decided to explore the world of porn when he realized he lived only ten minutes from the San Fernando Valley—the epicenter of American porn films. Yngvesson presents an unbiased look at the business of porn and interviews many well-known stars, including Jeanna Fine, Sean Micheals, Steven St. Croix, Brooke Waters and many more.

THE SECRET LIVES OF ADULT STARS (2004) Some of the biggest names in the porn industry star in this documentary. Watch as they discuss how they got into the business and take an inside look into the adult industry. A lot of the top stars of the 1990s are interviewed, including the lovely Julia Ann, the super-sexy Juli Ashton, the always adorable Asia Carrera, frisky Felecia, smoking hot Kylie Ireland and the goddess Nina Hartley.

TCM ARCHIVES - FORBIDDEN HOLLYWOOD, COLLECTION 1-3: Go back in time with this collection of pre-Code Hollywood films and see how naughty they were before the Wills Hays Code. There are a lot of great forgotten films in this series, including *Baby Face*—with Barbara Stanwyck as a man-hating gold-digger (look for John Wayne in a supporting role). Also included in this collection: the adulterous *The Divorcee* and the fun role-reversal *Female*, in which a 1930s female executive has as many men as she wants!

NAUGHTY HISTORY

THE PEOPLE VS. LARRY FLYNT (1996) A Golden Globe nominee for Best Performance by an Actor and Actress (Woody Harrelson and Courtney Love) and winner for Best Screenplay and Director. This is an inspiring tale of free speech as manifested in the adult entertainment industry. It also highlights the troubling hypocrisy of how violence in media is given a pass while nudity and sex is deemed inappropriate.

HUGH HEFNER: AMERICAN PLAYBOY (1998) This was part of A&E's *Biography* series and includes interviews with Hef, Christine Hefner, Tony Curtis, Ray Bradbury and many others. It has a lot of sexy shots of Playmates, the infamous Mansion parties and plenty of torrid tales to keep you glued to the screen.

PLAYBOY: INSIDE THE PLAYBOY MANSION (2002) This little documentary has a lot of footage of some of the wild annual parties held at the Playboy Mansion. There are loads of pretty girls and interviews with people who frequent the parties, including Barbie Benton, Shannon Tweed and Pamela Anderson.

WONDERLAND (2003) John Holmes was famous in the '70s for his 14-inch penis and all the porn movies he made. *Wonderland* lets us step inside another, more dangerous world of Hollywood with John Holmes at the center of one of the most brutal crime scenes—the Wonderland Murders. Val Kilmer is excellent as the coke-addicted Holmes, as is Lisa Kudrow as his frazzled wife.

SEX IN FILMS

Hollywood has movies for everyone, including those who want something steamy. If you're looking for a ménage à trois or orgy tonight, then snuggle up on the couch with your lover and slip in one of the films listed below and see what happens. You don't have to watch porn to get turned on, as any one of these movies will do the trick. All the films listed here were filmed in L.A., but you can find more naughty movies by checking out the book *Erotic Cinema* by Douglas Keesey and Paul Duncan.

Erotica: *Gold Diggers of 1933* (1933) is one of the best, sexiest musicals you'll ever see. It features Joan Blondell, Aline MacMahon and Ruby Keeler as three bombshells trying to stage a Broadway musical after being shut down because of overdue bills.

Femme Fatale: *Mata Hari* (1931) features one of Hollywood's greatest of all time—Greta Garbo—in the title role as the exotic dancer who was rumored to be a German spy during World War I. Lionel Barrymore is his usual excellent self, and Ramon Novarro is Garbo's hunk of choice (who can blame her?).

Sex Goddess: *The Outlaw* (1943) brings you Jane Russell in Howard Hughes's sexy western that brought him a lot of grief from Hollywood censors. It's easy to see why this film rankled the censors' feathers. Jane Russell busts out all over in the film and commands your attention for every second she's on screen.

Nudity: *10* (1979), starring Dudley Moore, Julie Andrews and the gratuitously nude Bo Derek, is a fun social-commentary comedy directed by Blake Edwards (Julie Andrews's husband). Dudley Moore, suffering a midlife crisis, spies Bo Derek on a beach and becomes fascinated by her enough to follow her to Mexico. Who wouldn't be tempted to follow her and that lovely body?

Fellatio and Cunnilingus: *Color of Night* (1994) with Bruce Willis is a weird psychological thriller / serial killer movie. Willis plays a psychologist who's losing his patients one by one to an unknown killer. If that's not enough to bring you in, how about Willis and Jane March having sex in a pool where he goes down on her and vice versa? Or Miss March having lesbian sex and being completely nude?

NAUGHTY HISTORY

Hunk: *American Gigolo* (1980) has Richard Gere as the title man who gives a hand (and much more) to Lauren Hutton—the wife of a prominent politician. Gere soon finds himself framed for a murder that is heavy on S&M themes, and Hutton is his only alibi. How can he ask her to give him the alibi when that will reveal their affair and ruin her life?

Ménage à Trois: *Rebel Without a Cause* (1955) features one that's never consummated on screen, but is evident for anyone to see if they wish. James Dean (who was rumored to swing from both sides of the batter's box in real life) plays Jim Stark in this iconic role. His on-screen pal, Plato (Sal Mineo), has the 1955 version of the hots for him. Throw Natalie Wood as the sultry Judy into the mix and you're ready for plenty of underlying three-way action.

Orgy: *Zabriskie Point* (1970), Michelangelo Antonioni's weird take on 1960s American counterculture, features a wild orgy scene in Death Valley that features members of the Open Theatre performance art group that was so realistic that the film was investigated to see if its creators violated the Mann Act (passed in 1910 to protect the transportation of females for the purpose of prostitution, human trafficking or illegal sexual acts).

Naughty Travel

Welcome to L.A.

PLANNING YOUR TRIP

LOCALS: There's so much more to L.A. than just shopping, going to the beach or hanging out with friends at your favorite neighborhood café. If you haven't already, why not get out and explore the naughty side of your city? Who knows, there may be something naughty waiting in your neighborhood bookstore or lingerie shop that you walk by every day. Plan a day or a weekend to explore on your own, with your friends or your lover(s). Still unsure of where to begin? Don't worry. This book will help open up a side to L.A. you never knew.

VISITORS: This book is great for those of you planning a week or weekend getaway in L.A. Whether this is your first, second or tenth visit, make this your first naughty one. I will show you how to make the most of your trip, as I know all the naughty secrets to L.A. I've done the groundwork for you and had to take a few for the team. It was a tough job, but

NAUGHTY GIRL'S GUIDE TO LOS ANGELES

someone had to spend countless days and nights out on the town finding you the naughtiest entertainment, kinkiest lingerie stores and sexiest bars and restaurants. Now I want you to come along for a wild ride.

LOS ANGELES NAUGHTY TRAVEL BOOKS

- *Horny? Los Angeles* By Jessica Hundley and Jon Alain Guzik
- *L.A. Bizarro: The All-New Insider's Guide to the Obscure, the Absurd, and the Perverse in Los Angeles* By Anthony Lovett and Matt Maranian

WHAT TO PACK

L.A. is a very laid-back city when it comes to dress. Yes, we may be known for celebrity award shows such as the Oscars where guests are dressed to the nines; but when the cameras are off Los Angeleans like to wear comfortable "L.A. casual" clothing, such as jeans, tank tops and flip-flops. Just make sure to pair your casual look with designer sunglasses and a handbag, as it's "so L.A." to meld the casual and the chic.

It's hard to tell who has money in this city, as the people who have money dress the most casual. Even when going out at night, most Los Angeleans dress up by wearing their best jeans with heels, a sexy top and a designer bag. There are a few of us who still dress to impress when heading out on the town in L.A., so feel free to look sharp.

Pack some of your favorite jeans, tank tops, sexy heels, sandals, cute sundresses and at least one sexy dress for nighttime. Even though we're a casual city, everyone has his or her own style, so bring yours with you.

YOUR NAUGHTY SUITCASE

When packing for your trip to L.A., be sure to leave some room or bring an extra bag for stuff to make your naughty vacation a little extra sinful. If you're not sure what you should bring to spice things up, don't fret. Here you'll find information on everything from a discreet condom case to a Marilyn Monroe costume. You can visit the websites listed to buy the items before your trip or purchase them once you've arrived in L.A. Also, I have an online sex store where you can purchase all the items on the next few pages or choose from over 100,000 items at www.SiennaSinclaireSexShop.com.

NAUGHTY TRAVEL

JUST IN CASE
www.justincaseinc.com

Anyone coming to L.A. needs to pack condoms "just in case." These days you can't depend on the guy to have condoms, so be responsible and safe by carrying your own. With the ready availability of condoms, it's silly and dumb to not have them on hand. So carry your condoms in a discreet, glamorous case by Just in Case, who's located in L.A.

ADULT TOY BOX BRIEFCASE
For Your Nymphomation
www.foryournymphomation.com

These briefcases are great to store all your sex toys and keep them organized when traveling. It's very discreet and comes with a lock, so you can use it as a carry-on or leave it out in your hotel room. No one will know what's inside it, except the person running the X-ray machine at the airport, so you might get a few confused looks or smiles. Or it can fit perfectly in your suitcase while keeping all your sex toys organized in one container. They come in fun colors such as purple, pink and red—or you can choose the leopard design.

SWIMSUITS
Beach Bunny Swimwear
136 S. Robertson Blvd., Mid-City West
310.858.8588
www.beachbunnyswimwear.com

This store has the sexiest and most amazing swimsuits in all of L.A. It's like wearing lingerie or bringing your boudoir to the beach. They sell more than just swimsuits, as you'll find sexy lounge wear, matching towels, sandals, jewelry and much more. They are constantly expanding their brand, so you never know what new items you'll find. Plus they have a convenient location near all the great stores on Robertson Blvd., so make sure to pay them a visit before heading to the beach or lounging poolside.

SCREAMING O STUDIO COLLECTION
Screaming O
www.screamingo.com

Don't leave home without Screaming O's new Studio Collection of cheeky cosmetic sex toys. Their Studio Collection has a vibrating blush brush, mascara wand and lipstick along with compacts and lip glosses that are actually warming and cooling gels. You can carry all of your naughty toys in their "Chic and Discreet Studio Makeup Purse." Put this cosmetic bag in your carry-on along with your sex toys when you're heading out for a flight and security won't even know. And what better way to relax during a long flight than by "freshening up" in the restroom with the contents of your bag?

NAUGHTY NECESSITIES KIT
Pleasure Chest
7733 Santa Monica Blvd., West Hollywood
323.650.1022
www.thepleasurechest.com

If you aren't sure what sexy things to bring, or if you haven't bought any yet, then this naughty kit might be right for you. It comes in a perfect travel-size case that you can pack away in your suitcase, carry-on or adult toy box briefcase. It's perfect for the solo traveler, as it comes with a mini-vibrator for those nights when you'd rather turn on the hotel-room porn and give yourself a treat. It also contains condoms for when you get lucky. Or, for a girls' getaway, you can share some of the items inside. There's enough in this kit to go around.

DELUXE DOOR JAM KIT
Pleasure Chest
7733 Santa Monica Blvd., West Hollywood
323.650.1022
www.thepleasurechest.com

Hotel-room towels and sheets only provide limited options for bondage, so be sure to pack these quick and easy-to-use restraints. Just place the straps under and over any door in the hotel room and firmly close it. The set comes with two pairs of adjustable cuffs and four door jam straps for wrists and ankles. It doesn't come with a blindfold or whip, but what else are those extra towels for anyway?

NAUGHTY TRAVEL

NAUGHTY LOS ANGELES SOUVENIRS
Naughty Girl Travel Store
http://www.cafepress.com/thenaughtygirlsstore

If you want to proclaim your status as a "Naughty Travel Girl," a "L.A. Naughty Girl," or a "Naughty Girl" (or all three!), check out my CafePress store for all sorts of naughty merchandise. I offer t-shirts, thongs, travel mugs, bags, iPhone and iPad covers and more for all your naughty travel needs. So make sure to visit my website before or after your trip to L.A. to get your naughty Los Angeles souvenirs.

BOOTY PARLOR
www.bootyparlor.com

This is an amazing website where you'll find tons of girly and naughty products for a night of solo pleasure, pampering yourself or a sexy date night with your lover. The products are amazing and they smell so good! Design a "lovekit" by choosing the products you want before heading to L.A. so you can feel extra sexy when hitting the town. You can also purchase Booty Parlor's book "Mojo Makeover," which is a four-week makeover to a sexier you. You can do the makeover before heading to L.A. to get your "mojo" back or while you're here on your naughty holiday.

PLAYBOY BUNNY COSTUME
Trashy Lingerie
402 N. La Cienega Blvd., West Hollywood
www.trashy.com

Remember when you found your Dad's or your brother's *Playboy* magazines in their top dresser drawer? Maybe you've always wanted to dress up as a *Playboy* bunny and have your lover take frisky photos of you. Or you've been intrigued by those photos of *Playboy* mansion parties and want to put together a girlfriends party with a *Playboy* theme. Either way, you can make your vampy Playmate fantasies come true with anyone of Trashy's sexy bunny costumes.

MARILYN COSTUME
Ursula Costumes
2516 Wilshire Blvd., Santa Monica
310.582.8230
www.ursulascostumes.com

She seduced a U.S. President and his brother. She seduced Elvis, the Rat Pack, Joe DiMaggio, and, without much effort, the rest of the world. Every woman wanted to be her and every man (and many women) wanted to have her. With this outfit you can walk into the room and sing "Happy Birthday" to your lover, pose for a sexy cheesecake photo shoot or let your lover direct you in a sexy movie scene that perhaps leads to even sexier action. Tap into your inner Marilyn Monroe and let your glamorous fantasies loose.

SECRET RENDEZVOUS

Choosing the perfect hotel can be just as important as deciding what sexy outfit to wear out on the town. The number of hotels, motels and bed-and-breakfasts in L.A. is astounding, so choosing where you're going to stay can be difficult. The easiest way to begin sorting through all the choices is to determine what you're looking to do here.

For example, if you want to come to L.A. for the beaches and oiled-up sexy bodies, then stay in hotels near the beach. Don't stay in Beverly Hills or Hollywood, as those areas are far away from the beaches and don't give you easy access to them either. L.A. is not an easy city to get around, whether you have a car or not, so stay in the area where you plan on spending the majority of your vacation. Remember that there is always traffic in L.A.—always.

The next thing to consider when planning your trip is the size of your party. Are you coming solo and looking for a hotel where you can meet

people and maybe get lucky? Are you planning a girls' getaway and want to be near all the erotic shopping, cafés and clubs? Or do you want somewhere exclusive and naughty for you and your lover to have a wild weekend that you'll remember for years? Don't worry. There are plenty of sexy hotels, that I've personally chosen, for you to stay and play on the next few pages.

SOLO GETAWAY

VICEROY
1819 Ocean Ave., Santa Monica
310.260.7500
www.viceroyhotelsandresorts.com

This beautiful hotel is great if you're looking for a trendy hotel near the beach. The Viceroy Santa Monica is great for mingling. On weekends the Cameo Bar downstairs (just off the lobby) is always packed with lots of eye candy. If it's a warm night, head out to the poolside bar. This is a very trendy hotel for anyone who is traveling solo and looking to meet people. It's an all-in-one hotel where you can sleep, dine, drink and mingle. It's close to the Ocean Front Walk, Main Street (with all kinds of neat shops) and the 3rd Street Promenade's stores, restaurants and bars.

MONDRIAN HOTEL
8440 Sunset Blvd., West Hollywood
800.785.2179
www.mondrianhotel.com

West Hollywood is the place to be if you're visiting L.A. It's where all the hotspots are located, plus you're very close to tons of shopping, cafés, clubs and some of the best restaurants. The Mondrian is right in the middle of all the action. It's a high-fashion hotel that caters to the glitterati and it boasts some of the best views of the city from the upper floors. This is the perfect hotel for a solo traveler as you get access to Sky Bar, which can be very hard to get into if you're not a hotel guest. The Mondrian is the place to see and be seen. You will not be solo very long at this hotel if you play your cards right.

MAISON 140
140 S Lasky Dr., Beverly Hills
310.281.4000
www.maison140beverlyhills.com

This gorgeous boutique hotel is for the solo traveler who wants a more intimate setting. Maison 140 features French and Asian themes and has only 43 rooms. This is the hotel to live out a nice European film noir fantasy. Their lounge, Bar Noir, is tucked away in the lobby and is the perfect place for you to grab a cocktail while mingling with some of the locals. Make sure to try their signature cocktail, the French Kiss. Also, you're only two blocks away from world-class shopping on Rodeo Drive and other high-end stores on Wilshire Boulevard.

— NAUGHTY TRAVEL —

W HOTEL
930 Hilgard Ave., Westwood
310.208.8765
www.whotels.com/LosAngeles

W Hotels are known for the culture scenes around them, and the one in Westwood has one of the best. It's right in the middle of Westwood, which is located next to UCLA and a very cute shopping area. Dining at their restaurant, Ninethirty, puts you right in the middle of the hotel's bar scene, so it's a great place to people watch, mingle and make new friends. This hotel has an amazing bar—Whiskey Blue—which can be busy on some weekdays, but it's the place to be on the weekends. As a guest you get access to Whiskey Blue, not an easy feat on weekends.

W HOTEL

THE HUNTLEY HOTEL

— NAUGHTY TRAVEL —

GIRLS' GETAWAY

THE HUNTLEY HOTEL
1111 2nd St., Santa Monica
310.394.5454
www.thehuntleyhotel.com

This hotel has one of my favorite restaurants, The Penthouse. It overlooks the Pacific Ocean from eighteen stories high. I love the all-white décor and the bar's chocolate martinis. This is the perfect hotel to stay with your girlfriends, as it's only a few blocks from the beach and the 3rd Street Promenade—where you'll find all the shops, cafés, restaurants and bars you can handle. This hotel is "where modern beachside glamour meets casual urban chic." You'll get a perfect feel of what beach life is like in L.A., with a mix of "sea and city, and casual and chic."

BEVERLY WILSHIRE
9500 Wilshire Blvd., Beverly Hills
310.275.5200
www.fourseasons.com/beverlywilshire

What girl hasn't watched *Pretty Woman* with envy, especially when Julia Roberts went on her Rodeo Drive shopping spree? Stay at this glamorous, famous hotel and you can live out your *Pretty Woman* fantasies. Even if you can't spend like Julia Roberts in the movie, you can still go window shopping or head one block over to South Beverly Drive, where you can find more affordable shopping—along with cafés, restaurants and bars. Or maybe you and your girlfriends can have a luxurious day in the Beverly Wilshire spa, which incorporates themes and treatments from Europe and Asia. It's a great way to spend a day and get ready for a fun night.

HOLLYWOOD ROOSEVELT
7000 Hollywood Blvd., Hollywood
323.466.7000
www.hollywoodroosevelt.com

Step back into a bygone era of old Hollywood glamour at the hotel that hosted the inaugural Oscars. It's located in the perfect spot, as you're near all the naughty sex toy stores on Hollywood and Sunset Boulevards. On the weekends and all day Sunday, why not rent a cabana room poolside so that you can party all day and night at the Tropicana Bar? This bar is really popular during the warmer months and can be very hard to get into—if you're not a guest. Or head to Teddy's where glamour and celebrities come together for a private, late-night evening of, "What happened behind Teddy's bronze doors, never happened." But make sure to dress to the nines while staying at the Roosevelt, as this is one glamorous hotel where it pays to look the part.

L.A. SKY BOUTIQUE HOTEL
2352 Westwood Blvd., Westwood
310.474.4551
www.skyhotella.com

This glamorous, budget-friendly hotel is ideal for a girlfriends' getaway. Trust me, you will feel sexy staying at this hotel. It puts you close to trendy Westwood, which offers tons of affordable shopping, cafés, restaurants and bars. Westwood is a mix of frisky college students and sharp-dressed professionals. It's a very nice neighborhood surrounded by high-end, high-rise condominiums and million-dollar homes, but it's still affordable for the budget-conscious traveler.

LOVER'S GETAWAY

HOTEL BEL-AIR
701 Stone Canyon Rd., Bel Air
310.472.1211
www.hotelbelair.com

Tucked away in Bel Air Estates, this gorgeous hotel is quiet and removed from the hustle and bustle of L.A., yet close to Beverly Hills, Century City and Hollywood. It has an amazing 12-acre private sanctuary of hundreds of plants, flowers, trees and botanical wonders, along with an ethereal lake with swans. Stepping into this hotel and its grounds is like stepping into

THE MALIBU INN

another world. Since opening in the 1940s, the hotel has attracted many celebrities seeking privacy, including Grace Kelly, Cary Grant, Elizabeth Taylor and Marilyn Monroe. If you want a romantic, private getaway spot, you can't do much better than this.

CHANNEL ROAD INN
219 W. Channel Rd., Santa Monica
310.459.1920
www.channelroadinn.com

This charming, Southern-style B&B is a romantic retreat by the sea and at the end of Route 66. It's been voted the top bed-and-breakfast in Los Angeles on more than one occasion. Guests are pampered with sumptuous food, including wine and hors d'oeuvres in the afternoon. Many of the rooms have fireplaces, and you can also rent a room with a jetted spa for you and your lover to relax after a day of shopping at the Santa Monica farmers market, strolling the Santa Monica Pier or staying in bed all day.

THE MALIBU INN
22969 Pacific Coast Hwy., Malibu
310.456.1160
www.malibubeachinn.com

At the Malibu Inn "sex on the beach" isn't just a cocktail, it's a distinct possibility. The hotel is situated right on Carbon Beach, which is also known as "Billionaires' Beach." All rooms have ocean views and come stocked with seven bottles of wine from local vineyards. When booking your room you can request items such as chocolate-dipped fruit, rose petals on the bed or champagne delivered to your room when you arrive. You can have a romantic dinner on the beach or relax at the spa with ocean views. Also, the hotel is close to all the action. You can shop at the high-end Malibu Lumber Yard, hike through the many trails nearby, walk on the beach or dine at Duke's, Nobu or the famous Moon Shadows restaurant.

CHATEAU MARMONT
8221 Sunset Blvd., West Hollywood
323.656.1010
www.chateaumarmont.com

You will feel like a movie star when you stay at the famous Chateau Marmont. The hotel sits up on a hill and resembles a castle, so it seems like you're heading into a Fellini movie as you approach. This hotel is very discreet for those who want a private holiday. The Chateau Marmont has quiet, romantic areas inside and out for sipping on cocktails or you can head to Bar Marmont, which is open to the public. The Chateau Marmont invites you for a "martini, for the sex appeal, to make the deal—naughty or nice." Also, you're in walking distance to all the restaurants, stores, clubs and coffee shops.

NAUGHTY TRAVEL

KINKY GETAWAY

L.A. STAY AND PLAY
www.lastayandplay.com

As their website says: "Motel 6, it ain't." This is L.A.'s one and only fetish-themed rental space. It's the ultimate place to stay for a naughty vacation. If you want the ultimate kinky retreat for your next fetish event or weekend getaway, this is the place to go. Renting the space is a lot like renting a mountain cabin or summer cottage. There is no maid service (although it's stocked with fresh towels and linens) or transportation to and from the space, and you're expected to leave it "broom clean" (with the provided cleaning supplies).

L.A. Stay and Play is a 3,000-square-foot loft that is meant for one thing only: fetish play. The space has a queen-size bed, a loft bed and three sleeping cages with padded floors. You can wake up next to your darling little slave asleep at your feet in his or her cage ready to serve you for the whole day. The hotel is high on the wish list during the many fetish-themed events in L.A., so you need to book early if you're planning on staying here during one of them. Plus you can walk right out of the hotel in full fetish gear without anyone batting an eye.

The space has a big play area split into different themes and with furniture and BDSM equipment created by some of the world's top fetish designers. You can play doctor in the Medical Room, be treated like a queen in the

Gilded Parlor, unleash your inner naughty girl in the Scarlet Boudoir or push your slave to the limit in the Interrogation Station.

It's equipped with a full kitchen, so you can stock up on groceries, drinks and anything else you need for a long weekend without having to leave the hotel. However, if you do decide to get out L.A. Stay and Play is in the heart of L.A.'s art and fashion district and near plenty of fun stuff to see and do. It's also around the corner from a sexy bar called Bordello where the owners of L.A. Stay and Play hold their "Fade2Black" party during L.A.'s annual Kinkball Fetish Weekend.

Bring your lover, slave or Master to "stay and play" for a kinky getaway you'll always remember.

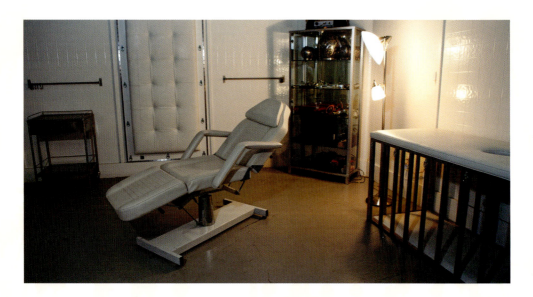

L.A. STAY AND PLAY

BEST PLACES FOR A SECRET RENDEZVOUS

There are a few things to consider when choosing a hotel for your secret rendezvous. First, any motel where you can just drive up to the door is ideal. The quicker you can get into your room, the quicker your clothes can hit the floor. Second, a hotel where you don't have to walk through the lobby is great because you don't have to worry about running into anyone you might not want to see or getting a curious look from the staff. Third, look for a hotel with an elevator that bypasses the front desk and takes you straight to your room. This also gives you a little time for a quick elevator warm-up for what's to come after you hang the "Do Not Disturb" sign on the door. Fourth, find a hotel you trust—preferably one with a discreet staff. You can usually find such people in high-end hotels. Make sure to tip well, and once you've found a hotel that respects and protects your privacy, stay a loyal customer.

Here are the two best hotels for private dalliances in Los Angeles:

AVALON HOTEL
9400 W. Olympic Blvd., Beverly Hills
310.277.5221
www.avalonbeverlyhills.com

This hotel can be very discreet if you stay in the rooms located in the back, as they are not attached to the hotel and have their own private entry door. Therefore, they're great for sneaking your lover (celebrity or not) into your room without anyone seeing. Maybe that naughty secret is you!

CHATEAU MARMONT
8221 Sunset Blvd., Hollywood
323.656.1010
www.chateaumarmont.com

Harry Cohn, founder of Columbia Studios, was often quoted as saying, "If you must get in trouble, do it at the Chateau Marmont." This very discreet and exclusive Hollywood hotel was built in 1929. Anyone looking to get the scoop on a Hollywood scandal will have a tough job here. First, they have to get past the valet, who will not let anyone in unless they are a guest, friend of a guest or eating at the restaurant. This way no one can just walk into the lobby and get a glimpse of who's in there. Once inside, there are only two elevators and a staircase, so you can easily sneak in your lover by taking one of the elevators straight to your room. You don't have to walk through a lobby where people might see you. Another added bonus

NAUGHTY TRAVEL

is that this hotel has a strict camera policy. If they see you taking photos they will approach you to see if you're a guest of the hotel. This policy is enforced so well that most people know it's frowned-upon to take photos. The Chateau is a great place to get away and not be noticed by prying eyes.

FINDING A DATE

Why not set up a date or a few dates while planning your trip to L.A.? Or maybe you already live here and are looking to try something different. Either way, if you're looking to meet new people or find a date, check out Los Angeles Magazine at http://dating.lamag.com or SingularCity at http://singularcity.com.

As their website says, "SingularCity is an online meeting place for successful single men and women living in Los Angeles who lead happy, productive, fulfilling lives. The members of our singular community are active professionals, creative types and those interested in finding like-minded individuals to share online and offline activities, events and friendship. Whether your interest is travel, sports, the arts, dining, wines, entertainment, philosophy, self-improvement, relationships, the economy or single parenting, you'll find a group for you."

NAUGHTY TRAVEL

The site has groups devoted to wine, film, dance, travel and more. It offers a lot of advice columns on dating and the single life. You can find information on special events like holiday-themed parties and yoga classes for singles, so it's easy to find someone with your interests and even a party where you can meet several like-minded people.

MOTEL FETISH

I love motels. They seem to have this kinky energy that gets into you as soon as you step into the room. L.A. has tons of motels, and some even rent by the hour for those who like quickies. On the next page are some motels that are close to shopping, museums, clubs and restaurants. For those who want to step back in time and experience old Hollywood, you can stay in a motel where many celebrities have stayed for some of their secret rendezvous. Who knows, maybe you'll become that rendezvous!

Motels serve a great purpose for those who want to be discreet. You can drive up to your room without having to walk through a lobby and your car is right there if you need to make a quick run for condoms, wine or a ball gag. Motels are very popular with escorts in Los Angeles because they can rent rooms by the hour for their clients who don't want to be seen, or who have to get back to the office.

NAUGHTY GIRL'S GUIDE TO LOS ANGELES

Another thing I love about motels is that they're more likely to have free naughty amenities. For example, many motels have ceiling and wall mirrors for added visual stimulation. And some rooms have hot tubs in them where the jets can be used for getting you off. Also, their furniture is usually heavy and/or bolted down, to prevent theft, making them great props for tying up your lover.

There are so many naughty things you can do in a motel room, so let your imagination run wild by planning an evening of kinky fun with your lover.

NAUGHTY TRAVEL

CORAL SANDS MOTEL
1730 N. Western Ave., Hollywood
323.467.5141
www.coralsands-la.com

What makes this cute motel naughty are the mirrors hung next to the beds so that you can see yourself during your frisky romps. It's also gay friendly, so if your girlfriends' getaway is a little playful, no one will mind.

SAHARAN MOTOR HOTEL
7212 W. Sunset Blvd., Hollywood
323.874.6700
www.saharanhotel.com

I used this motel for a naughty photo shoot once, as they have great rooms if you're looking for that real motel look. Upgrade to the suite and you'll get a hot tub surrounded with mirrors for some kinky fun.

SEA SHORE MOTEL
2637 Main St., Santa Monica
310.392.2787
www.seashoremotel.com

This place, just two blocks from Santa Monica Beach, is great for those who are looking for sex on the beach or a place to take that hottie you met on the beach after fun in the sun. Plus it's located on historical Main Street, which is home to an eclectic collection of restaurants, boutiques and cafés, including California's first Starbucks and Ben & Jerry's.

SNOOTY FOX MOTOR INN
4120 S. Western Ave., Los Angeles
323.294.0083
www.snootyfoxmotorinn.com

This motel with a fun name has old-school décor, which is hard to find nowadays with most motels remodeling. You'll feel like you're living out a photo shoot from a vintage copy of *Swank* or *Oui* when you stay here. Plus they have huge mirrors over the bed and on the ceilings! You can't get any better than that for an hour or a whole night of fun.

VIBE MOTEL
5922 Hollywood Blvd., Hollywood
323.469.8600
www.vibehotel.com

Formerly known as the "Movie Town Motel," this motel, built in 1952, was a rendezvous spot for up-and-coming actors and actresses in the late 1950s and early 1960s. It's been remodeled since the glamorous days of old Hollywood, but it's still a secret rendezvous for many.

NAUGHTY TIP #1

MOTEL RENDEZVOUS

Why not spice up your sex lives by trying something different with you and your lover at a motel? If you're not sure what to do, plan a night at one of the motels I mentioned, pages 91-92, and make it naughty by acting out the following fantasy.

"Call Girl Fantasy"

Don't lie. You've thought of this, and you know your lover probably has, too. You've wondered what it would be like to dress up as a call girl and show up at your lover's motel room. You and your lover can do it without worrying about the possibility of a vice cop getting into the mix (which, on second thought, might be fun).

To act out your fantasy, start by wearing something really sexy and naughty. Think Julia Roberts in *Pretty Woman*, Kathleen Turner in *Crimes of Passion* or Theresa Russell in *Whore*. Wear ripped nylons, knee-high boots, a skimpy skirt and a shirt with your bra showing. If you feel a little uncomfortable walking around in your skimpy outfit before you show up to the motel, then wear a sexy trench coat. As he opens the door, slowly reveal what you have hidden underneath your coat.

Once you've rented a room, it's time to set the scene. The room does most of the work for you, but feel free to add a vintage ashtray, matchbook, mini bottles of liquor and rocks glasses if you want more of a retro motel feel. Put a flyer next to the phone with your number on it. Or, if you plan ahead, you can print out a sexy flyer with your photo on it and write: "For a Good Time Call [your name here]." Next, go somewhere and wait for your lover to call you. You might go to a nice bar nearby for a drink to calm your nerves, because you may be squirming in your seat as you imagine your lover entering the room and finding your flyer. When he calls, he'll ask what "services" you provide. You can go on to describe the things that you'll do to him when you show up at his motel room.

Show up at your rented room where your lover is waiting and knock. Once he answers, greet him with, "Hi, I'm Candy!" or any fake name you or he would like. If you know he has a crush on a movie star or still dreams about his high school German teacher you could use any of those names.

Walk past him and move to the bed. Open up your purse that you have stocked with all your naughty toys, lubes and condoms. You could take out

NAUGHTY TRAVEL

your handcuffs, dangle them on your finger while looking at your lover, and then ask, "What would you like to do?" Let both of your imaginations run wild.

If he "booked" you for the hour, make sure that you only stay for the hour to make the fantasy more real. Once the hour is up, get up, put your clothes back on, take your well-earned cash (if that's part of the game) and leave. You can leave for a minute and then come back if you're staying there the whole night or he can meet you back at your "real" hotel or your house if you live in L.A.

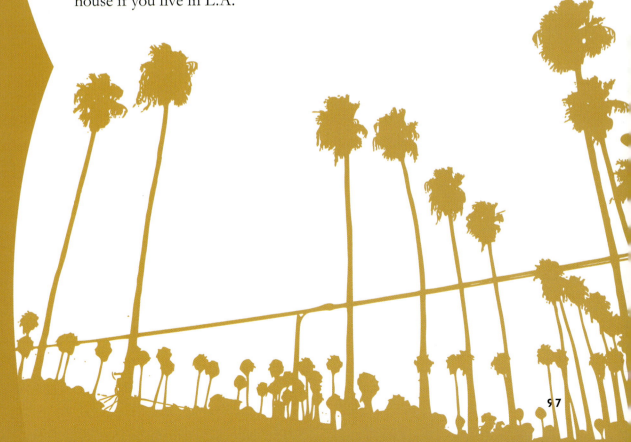

Naughty by Day

THE BODY SHOP

NAUGHTY DAY TOURS

Anyone can lounge on the beach or find their way to the Hollywood sign. You're not just anyone. You're reading this book because you want to know about the other side of L.A. that most people don't get to see—the naughty side.

If you've made it this far through the book, I'm guessing you're more than a bit of a libertine and that you enjoy a naughty vacation from time to time. Plus, you don't travel to a new town and eat at Burger King. You like to eat at neighborhood restaurants to get a taste of local flavor. You don't visit a new place and shop at the same stores that you have back home. Instead, you look for unique lingerie stores so that you can add select pieces to your risqué collection. And you don't visit a new place to see the same movie that's playing back home. You look for the nearest burlesque show or strip club. For you, packing condoms is as important as packing your toothbrush. And packing your sexiest lingerie before you leave for a new city is as crucial as checking the status of your flight.

You're looking for a sexy, hedonistic vacation where you want to get lucky. You know that getting there is half the fun, but the other half can be wild pleasure once you get there. So plan a naughty day tour for you and your lover, or just yourself. L.A. is full of beautifully debauched places that aren't hard to find if you know where to look. I'll be your naughty tour guide and travel agent.

One thing to consider before we get too far into making your travel plans—book early. A lot of kinky events and shows sell out quickly. Hotel space can become as rare as that perfect guy you're looking for. You don't want to get to town and have to stay on the opposite side of the city from where your juicy event is taking place. Plus booking early also helps you save money on flights and room rates.

THINGS TO SEE

DR. SUSAN BLOCK SHOW
www.drsusanblock.com
If you do only one thing in L.A., then this is the place to visit. You have to become a member, but once you have access it's as if you stepped into

PLAYBOY STUDIO

another world—one where all your erotic fantasies can come to life. Come for drinks and watch her live show, where she features different porn stars every Saturday night. You never know what's going to happen on her show or during her after-parties, so come prepared to play.

PLAYBOY STUDIO
2112 Broadway Ave., Santa Monica

This is Playboy's Santa Monica studio location where lots of hopeful Playmates come for test shots. A lot of beautiful women, world-famous photographers and glitterati have walked in and out of its doors. Most

FLYNT BUILDING

people, even locals, wouldn't even know it's there unless you looked over while driving by and saw the small Playboy bunny logo on the building.

THE CHELSEA LATELY SHOW
http://on-camera-audiences.com/shows/Chelsea_Lately

Be a guest for some naughty laughs with the cute-as-a-button Chelsea Handler. She's a best-selling author and has one of the sharpest wits on the planet. She's not afraid to call out TV and movie stars on their bad behavior and frankly talk about sex. Plan in advance so you can get a spot on the show by signing up on the website above.

FLYNT BUILDING
8484 Wilshire Blvd., Beverly Hills
www.flyntbuilding.com

The famous Hustler Building definitely stands out on its corner of La Cienega and Wilshire Boulevard. It's a tall structure in a heavily trafficked area of town, but no one seems to care. Larry Flynt's office is located here and young hopefuls go here to test for Flynt's various adult magazines and videos.

ANGELYNE BILLBOARDS
If you drive around L.A. enough, you're bound to see a billboard advertising a blonde with breasts spilling out of her pink lingerie. Her name

is Angelyne. No one really knows much about her. She's an occasional movie actress and has done a little TV work, but everyone knows her as the busty blonde on the billboards. Also, keep your eyes peeled for her famous pink Corvette around town.

PLACES TO VISIT

PROSTITUTION BOULEVARD
7200-7800 Sunset Blvd., Hollywood

Located on Sunset Boulevard between Fairfax and La Brea, this is Hollywood's red light district. Hugh Grant became even more famous for his midnight romp on these streets. Don't get in trouble here. You don't want to ruin your naughty vacation, but you can still see what's on the menu without buying.

HOLLYWOOD MUSEUM
1660 N. Highland Ave., Hollywood
323.464.7776
www.thehollywoodmuseum.com

Set in the massive, art deco structure of the old Max Factor Building, the Hollywood Museum has four floors and over 35,000 square feet of exhibits. You can see vintage makeup products from famous

NAUGHTY BY DAY

Hollywood starlets, costumes from an amazing amount of movies, classic cars and creepy stuff from horror films in the basement. Once a year they exhibit an amazing Marilyn Monroe display that contains over 200 items, including dresses, movie costumes and stunning photographs.

CHATEAU MARMONT
8221 Sunset Blvd., West Hollywood
323.656.1010
www.chateaumarmont.com

The "castle on the hill" hotel is famous for the Hollywood trysts that have taken place there. It is the place to have a secret rendezvous. The staff prides itself on the privacy of the guests and the hotel is built to keep your dealings—business or pleasure—secret. You can get inside to take a look around by booking dinner reservations or one of their many rooms, suites or bungalows. Or maybe you'll get lucky

HOLLYWOOD MUSEUM

NAUGHTY GIRL'S GUIDE TO LOS ANGELES

and be brought to the hotel to take place in a Hollywood tryst of your own.

HUSTLER HOLLYWOOD STORE
8920 West Sunset Blvd., West Hollywood
310.860.9009
www.hustlerhollywood.com

This "Barnes and Noble of porn" (as we locals often call it) is located on Sunset Boulevard. They have their own "walk of fame" with porn-star names such as Jenna Jameson, Ron Jeremy and the late, great Marilyn Chambers. They also have a nice café and free underground parking. The staff is helpful and the place is clean and tasteful. You can find everything here, from naughty coffee mugs to high-end vibrators.

THE BODY SHOP
8250 Sunset Blvd., West Hollywood
323.656.1401
www.bodyshophollywood.com

The Body Shop achieved world fame in the 1980s when it was used as a location for "Girls, Girls, Girls," Motley Crue's metal love song about

HUSTLER HOLLYWOOD STORE

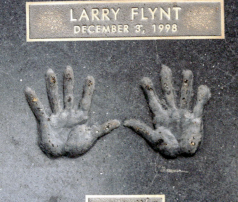

HUSTLER HOLLYWOOD STORE

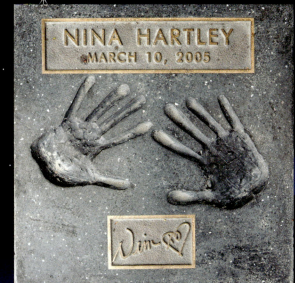

strip clubs. Motely Crue named the Body Shop as one of their favorite strip clubs in the 1987 hit song. A lot of movie stars and musicians have been here to either get or give a lap dance. Courtney Love was one of the many women trying to break into showbiz who worked there. It's rumored that Demi Moore trained there for her role in *Striptease*. In its early years the featured performers were big-time burlesque acts such as Betty Rowland and the legendary Lili St. Cyr. It was recently remodeled after a fire and features a lot of lovely, all-natural girls.

NAUGHTY BY DAY

TIKI THEATER
5462 Santa Monica Blvd., Hollywood
323.466.4264

This is the last stag theatre in L.A. to show only straight porn. It's a small place, and actually still has a turnstile in the entrance. Admission is cheap, but be prepared for a lot of guys who may not be content with keeping their hands to themselves. Then again, if that sounds like a good time, this might make for an interesting night. It's under new ownership and a lot of the old seats have been replaced with better ones. This place may not be your cup of tea, but it's part of L.A.'s naughty history and worth a visit as nudie theaters are on their way out in this city.

STUDS THEATRE
7734 Santa Monica Blvd., West Hollywood
323.650.9951

Studs is the last theatre of its kind, making it a must-see as it may not be here forever. It's an old stag theatre across the street from the Pleasure

Chest adult toy store. The Pussycat Theaters were upscale porn theatres known for their nice interiors and their famous cat-girl logo. But now it mostly shows gay porn with only one room dedicated to straight porn. They were among the first theatres to show *Deep Throat*. The first Pussycat Theater opened its doors in March 1966 on 444 South Hill Street in downtown L.A. Sadly, it's no longer there. By 2001 all the theaters were lost except this one. Today, the last Pussycat Theatre, renamed "Studs," is owned and run by Jonathan Cota—lover to the late George Tate, who was one of the two original owners of the Pussycat Theater chain. Studs has the handprints of famous porn stars out front. You need to get out on foot or you may miss this. John Holmes cemented his hand- and footprints there on February 7, 1985. Other porn stars immortalized here are Harry Reems, Jay Lawrence, Linda Lovelace, Marilyn Chambers, Eric Edwards, Kay Parker and Georgina Spelvin.

JEAN HARLOW'S HOUSE

NAUGHTY HOME TOUR

HEIDI FLEISS'S HOUSE
1270 Tower Grove Road, Beverly Hills

This is the house in which Heidi Fleiss ran a brothel frequented by the rich and famous. It is said that Madam Fleiss catered to many celebrities and politicians here. When asked to name names, she said it "wasn't her style." So remember, when in Hollywood you shouldn't kiss and tell.

JEAN HARLOW'S HOUSE
512 N. Palm Drive, Beverly Hills

This was the last home of Jean Harlow, an actress and sex symbol of the 1930s. The blond bombshell was taken from here to the hospital, where she died of renal failure on June 07, 1937 while only 26 years old.

NOTE: All the homes listed are private properties. Therefore, be respectful when driving by to check them out and no trespassing on their property.

--- NAUGHTY BY DAY ---

JOHN HOLMES – WONDERLAND HOUSE
8763 Wonderland Drive, Laurel Canyon

This is the site of the "Wonderland Murders," in which four people were beaten to death with a steel pipe on July 1, 1981. The people who lived at the Wonderland house allegedly broke into the house of Eddie Nash, a drug dealer. Nash allegedly retaliated by murdering them. It is also alleged that he had porn star John Holmes unlock the door to the Wonderland house. The major suspect in the case was Eddie Nash. But the best-known suspect was John Holmes, whose fingerprints were found at the house.

MARILYN MONROE'S LOVE PAD
625 Beach Road, Santa Monica

If you want to know how powerful the Rat Pack really were, look no further than this house. This was Peter Lawford's beach home in which Marilyn Monroe and President John F. Kennedy carried on their secret affair in the early 1960s. When the President needed to keep something quiet, he didn't go to the Secret Service. He went to the Rat Pack and this house.

MARILYN MONROE'S HOUSE
12305 Fifth Helena Drive, Brentwood

This is the only house Marilyn Monroe owned and it's where she died on August 4, 1962, at the age of 36. Her death will be forever known as one of the most famous, unsolved death scenes in Hollywood history.

MARILYN MONROE'S HOUSE

NAUGHTY GIRL'S GUIDE TO LOS ANGELES

HUGH HEFNER'S PLAYBOY MANSION
10236 Charing Cross Road, Beverly Hills

Hefner lives and runs his *Playboy* empire from this mansion, wearing his ubiquitous dressing gown and surrounded by beautiful girls. You've seen the videos and photos of the infamous parties. You've heard the stories. You've had the fantasies. Now if you could just slip past the gates . . . .

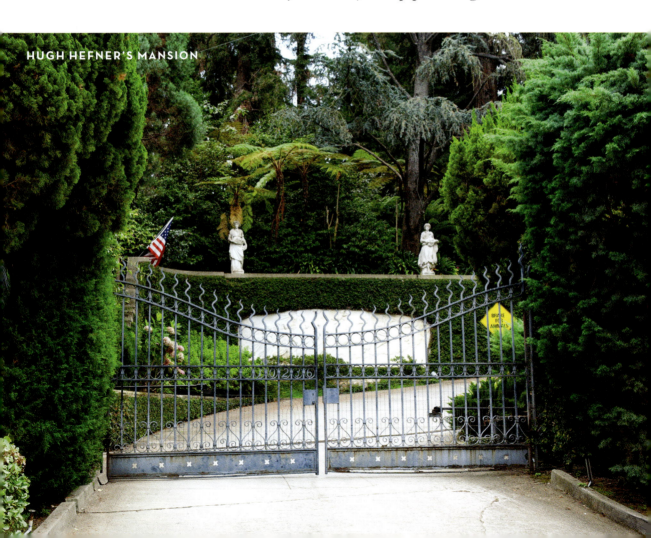

HUGH HEFNER'S MANSION

SEXY TOURS

Traveling to Los Angeles can be very intimidating, as the city offers so many choices that you may feel overwhelmed by all of them. If you're not sure where to begin, why not let me be your Naughty Tour Guide? As you'll soon figure out, I know where to find the hottest clubs, the sexiest restaurants, the kinkiest lingerie stores and the best places for naughty fun. I have three different travel packages to choose from, so call up your girlfriends and start planning.

THE EROTIC GIRL PACKAGE

Looking for a naughty getaway with your significant other or girlfriends? You can hire me as your sex coach to teach you one-on-one (or one-on-two?) lessons, take you shopping to the best sex stores in L.A., attend sex classes from well-known teachers and/or attend sexy parties at some of the hottest night clubs.

Not traveling to L.A. anytime soon but want to have an erotic night in another city of your choice? I have been to the best and naughtiest sex clubs, cafés, beaches, shops, shows, events and red light districts around the world. Let me help you plan your next naughty holiday. I can even help you pack for your holiday with naughty travel games to play with your lover, travel bags to carry all your toys and more.

THE PORN GIRL PACKAGE

A lot of people who come to L.A. have dreams of making it big as a movie star. Many of those dreams do come true, but instead of becoming a movie star they end up as a porn star. How would you like to see the naughty side of L.A. by visiting the set of a porn movie and an erotic photo shoot? L.A. is home to the porn industry, so why not see the naughtiest side of the city that most people will never see?

I will take you and your friends to a porn movie set for a behind-the-scenes look at how porn films are made. You will get a close-up look (sometimes very close!) at the filmmaking process and get to chat with the stars of the movie. You'll even get to take home a special behind-the-scenes video of your time on the set. It doesn't end there. You'll get tips to take home on how to make your own naughty video with your lover.

THE FETISH GIRL PACKAGE

Are you a fetishist visiting L.A. and would like to know all the hot spots in the fetish community? Are you looking to stay at a fetish hotel that can cater to all your kinky needs? This city has something for every kinkster. I can assist in planning your night out to fetish events or parties, introduce you to local kinksters and accompany you for a night or weekend (but don't be surprised if I lead you to the club by collar and chain). Also, I can take you shopping to all the fetish stores to help you pick out a fabulous latex or sexy outfit for the night.

You can learn more about my packages and booking them at: www.NaughtyTravelGirl.com

NAUGHTY EVENTS

You can always find something naughty to do in Los Angeles. So it's no surprise that Tinseltown can turn into Kinky-ville any day of the week. The city runs on sex and glamour. The movers and shakers in Hollywood expect only the best and that goes double for pleasures of the flesh.

So if you're coming to L.A. looking for a naughty fetish or adult industry event then you've come to the right city. You can go on a singles cruise to Mexico and get frisky with as many people as you like, or attend one of the adult shows here and chat with your favorite porn star. Or you can play dress-up with your lover or girlfriends by dressing up as a frisky pirate, fairy or medieval maiden, or getting kinky at a fetish event. As you can see, there are so many different events to choose from that you may never leave L.A.

RENAISSANCE FAIR
www.renfair.com/socal/

Located in the Santa Fe Dam Recreation Area, this is one of the biggest renaissance fairs in the country and lasts for over a month! You can watch jousting and swordfights, eat exotic foods, buy hand-crafted masks, or, better yet, check out all the hunky guys in armor and pretty girls in corsets that barely hide their breasts. Plus you can live out your medieval fantasies by dressing up and role playing with your lover.

ADULTCON
www.adultcon.com

This massive adult industry show is held at the L.A. Convention Center. All the major adult film stars show up, so it's a great way to meet a lot of people in the industry. And the vendors sell fun stuff for sexy single girls, including corsets, sex toys, lingerie, jewelry and a lot more.

GLAMOURCON
www.glamourcon.com

If you're looking to get into modeling, these shows are a great place to start. Many photographers, both professional and budding amateurs, come to the GlamourCon shows in search of new models. You can meet a lot of lovely ladies and get plenty of tips from them on how to get into the business. You might even be able to earn some extra money by being asked to an impromptu photography session!

NAUGHTY BY DAY

KANDY EVENTS
www.kandyevents.com

Kandy Events has four sexy parties every year. (1) Kandy Kruise is a cruise that leaves from L.A. to Mexico. The entire pool deck of the ship is turned into a massive nonstop party and is great for single's or girlfriends' getaway. (2) KandyLand is a wild party full of sexy treats that takes over the Roosevelt Hotel for the entire weekend. (3) Kandy Masquerade is your chance to live out your favorite scene from Eyes Wide Shut, as everyone there is masked and looking to indulge their naughty fantasies. You'll be amazed at all the lovely women wearing nothing but body paint and Victorian masks. (4) Kandy Halloween takes place at the Playboy Mansion every year and is one of their hottest parties. They have a 4,000 square-foot haunted house, spooky forests and graveyards, and hundreds of sexy girls and guys in wild costumes that will satisfy fantasies you didn't even know you had.

BUCCANEER DAYS
www.visitcatalinaisland.com/twoHarbors/Calendar.php

This pirate-themed event takes place on Catalina Island at Two Harbors. It's a wild party with thousands of attendees all dressed like pirates and wenches. There's plenty of partying here and everyone gets into the act. Bring your sexiest pirate outfit and shiver your timbers. And don't forget to bring your booty! You can learn more about them along with joining one of their Buccaneer Days Facebook groups by looking them up.

BOWLING FOR BOOBIES
www.bowlingforboobies.com

This fun breast cancer research fund raiser is held once a year in October at a bowling alley, so visit their website for location details and more. You and your girlfriends can form a team and have a great time with lots of fun people and sexy ladies bowling and raising money to find a cure for breast cancer.

L.A. TEMPTATIONS
www.lflus.com/latemptation/

The L.A. Temptations are Los Angeles' lingerie football team. Yes, you read that right. Who needs the Raiders, 49ers or Chargers when you can go to a Temptation game and watch gorgeous, hard-bodied women chasing and tackling each other? Take a trip to the Los Angeles Coliseum and check out women beautiful enough to be cheerleaders, but sexier than most cheerleaders hope to be. If you're looking for somewhere different to take your lover, then surprise him with a sexy football game.

LABYRINTH OF JARETH
www.labyrinthmasquerade.com

This wild masquerade event has some of the most amazing fantasy and steampunk costumes you'll ever see. You'll feel like you're in a J.R.R. Tolkien world at this party. If you fantasize about dancing with fairies, goblins, ghosts or Jules Verne-era scientists, you can live out your fantasy here.

LONG BEACH PRIDE
www.longbeachpride.com

Usually held in mid- to late May, the Long Beach Pride festival celebrates gay, lesbian, bisexual and transgender culture. It's the third-largest such celebration in the country. It brings in over 80,000 people over the weekend and has seven dance areas. The parade, which goes along Shoreline Drive, is something you don't want to miss. Save yourself a headache and pitch in for the guaranteed parking—it's only six bucks! Even if you're not gay or if you're just bi-curious, this is a fun festival to attend, as there is a lot going on throughout the weekend.

L.A. PRIDE
www.lapride.org

Mid-June brings L.A.'s massive gay pride weekend, which is full of events and an extravagant parade. The Friday-night DYKE March is a girls-only event, so gather your girlfriends for a night of fun—even if you don't swing that way. Don't miss out on Erotic City—a celebration of leather, kink, fetish and erotica as a fun part of life itself. You can see the outdoor dungeon, attend an erotic art show, watch bondage presentations and meet your favorite porn stars. This yearly event brings out all the frisky locals in L.A.

BELLY DANCER OF THE UNIVERSE COMPETITION
www.bellydanceroftheuniverse.com

This is a popular belly dancing competition that takes place in Long Beach every year. Hundreds, if not thousands, of people come to watch the amazing dancers, participate in classes or join in on group dances. You will see a lot of the world's best dancers and the hottest up-and-comers here.

ADULT INDUSTRY EVENTS

XBIZ LA
www.xbizla.com

Xbiz LA is an annual marketing event and trade show specializing in digital media and the adult entertainment industry. It's held once a year and is an amazing opportunity to meet the movers and shakers in the adult entertainment world. Plus, their after-parties are the best!

THE URBAN X AWARDS
www.urbanxawards.com

Showcasing the best black, Latino, Asian, BBW, gay, transsexual and interracial adult movies, performers and directors, this event is given the red-carpet treatment every year in front of a live audience at various clubs around L.A.

NAUGHTY BY DAY

FETISH EVENTS

KINKY PIRATE BALL
www.kinkypirateball.com

Held at the gorgeous El Rey Theatre, the Kinky Pirate Ball lets you live out your pirate-fetish fantasies. Even kinkier than Buccaneer Days, the Kinky Pirate Ball is sponsored by FetishMovies.com, so you know this won't be your average "Let's dress like pirates and get drunk on rum" party. They encourage you to wear your fetish gear and accessorize it with pirate flairs. They have fetish and latex fashion shows, erotic photography exhibits and a lot more.

L.A. KINK FETISH WEEKEND
www.lakinkfetishweekend.com/home

L.A. Kink Fetish Weekends are a four-day event held over Easter weekend. They have a massive party on each of the four days and celebrate everything from rubber fetish to big boobs. Every party has a strict dress code, so be sure to do your research on what to wear before you show up.

DOMCON LA
www.domconla.com

Calling itself the world's "premier professional and lifestyle domination convention," DomCon is held at the Hilton LAX every spring. They have a large exhibit hall with vendors, performances and seminars all day—and the Fetish Ball is not to be missed. Also, don't miss out on the informal Mistresses' Tea—which is ladies-only and a great way to meet professional and lifestyle dominatrices.

BONDAGE BALL
www.bondageball.com

Hollywood Bondage Ball is a fantastic event that hosts a variety of wild parties. One of their Halloween events was a "Ghostly Equestrian Ball," during which all kinds of lovely fetish gals got to ride on the backs of handsome slaves.

MASQUE DINNER
www.whatismasque.com/whatis.html

This is a fetish burlesque dinner show where people dress up like extras from *Eyes Wide Shut* and everyone wears a mask. The costumes are elaborate and it's a nice, relaxed atmosphere where you can meet like-minded people. The event is inspired by events in Amsterdam, so you know it's going to be an amazing, sensual experience. They have cocktails outside before the

NAUGHTY BY DAY

show starts. The food is surprisingly good for a dinner show and the performances are always naughty. Plus, they have an after-party at a private fetish studio where you can act out your naughty fantasies.

SEX ED CLASSES

Not everyone knows how to broach the subject of a threesome with their lover. And not everyone knows which dildo is best suited for them. But you can learn any sexual topic you want over the next few pages, as there are tons of sex educators in L.A. waiting to help you unleash your inner naughty girl.

So why not schedule some time for a sex class when you visit or try something different if you live here in L.A.? You can bring your lover or your girlfriends and make it a night of naughty fun! This section will provide you with opportunities for learning everything from how to tie a proper knot for bondage play to improved oral sex techniques. You can even learn how to be a dominant lover by taking some of the fetish classes listed. If that sounds appealing, then you might be a closet dominatrix who needs to bring that side of you out!

NAUGHTY CLASSES

PLEASURE CHEST
7733 Santa Monica Blvd., West Hollywood
323.650.1022
www.thepleasurechest.com

The Pleasure Chest offers a wide variety of sex education classes, including Anal Pleasure 101, Hardcore Sex, Impact Play, Tantra Sex and Blowjobs. Plus Jessica Drake, world-famous porn star, teaches her sex classes here. She only teaches about once a month and her classes fill up fast, so make sure to register online for any one of the workshops, or try them all as they're all FREE.

THE PLEASURE PARADIGM
www.thepleasureparadigm.com

Shama is a certified hypnotherapist, metaphysical teacher, healer and counselor. She teaches tantra sessions and workshops for you and your lover. She offers everything from Tantric basics to even more interesting sessions called Tickle Bath, Prostate Massage Ritual, Ejaculatory Mastery and Goddess Spot Massage Rituals. Check out her website to find out more about them and what she can do to spice up your sex life.

JAMYE WAXMAN
www.jamyewaxman.com

The Sex Educator for Generations X and Y, Jamye is one of the most well-known and sought-after lecturers in the field of human sexuality and relationships. She's a respected author and loves to teach. Her workshops, which usually run ninety minutes, cover topics such as how to talk to your partner, how to give better blow jobs and how to use sex toys. Also, you can tailor a workshop to fit your specific needs. She has no minimum attendance requirement and she'll answer any question you have.

DR. AVA CADELL
www.loveologyuniversity.com

Dr. Ava Cadell, known as the "loveologist to Hollywood stars," can teach you to become a "sexpert" in all things love. She offers tons of online courses for singles and couples or she can coach you one-on-one in her L.A. office. She firmly believes that lovemaking is an art that can be taught and learned.

LOU PAGET
www.loupaget.com

Developed by a woman for women, Dr. Paget offers seminars and books on becoming the lover you want to be. She offers a lot of courses in L.A., so make sure to check her schedule and then book in advance for your trip.

DR. PAT ALLEN
http://drpatallen.com/

Frank talk and straight-up advice from Dr. Allen is available in lectures, tele-seminars and books. You can also join one of her Monday-night seminars, where she'll take you on a "spiritual quest for more awareness on how to love one another." Or you can sign up for one of her many classes offered on her website.

DR. SUSAN BLOCK
www.drsusanblock.com

Visit here to learn everything you need to know about sex and more. Dr. Susan Block, who has been on the radio for over twenty-seven years, offers a free weekly radio show where you can tune in and listen to her guests give sex advice. You can also call in and ask questions or make a visit to her studio to watch her show live. Or you can hire her one-on-one for sex coaching 24/7, as she has a staff on hand at all hours of the day.

DAVID WYGANT
www.davidwygant.com

David Wygant is a world-renowned dating and relationship coach, author and speaker. Whether you live here or you're just visiting and want to become more confident with meeting and approaching men, David is the guy for you. He'll meet you one-on-one at a grocery store, gym, shopping mall, coffee shop or anywhere you want to practice picking up a guy.

SEX SURROGATE
www.sexsurrogateofla.com

Sex surrogates help people with sexual dysfunctions and phobias and feelings of inadequacy or lack of intimacy. Sessions are done with a therapist, the client and the surrogate. Tara Livingston is a certified sex surrogate, sex educator and healing massage practitioner who can help you develop social skills to make you a better date, learn more about your body and body image, discover true intimacy with your partner and much more.

REID ABOUT SEX
www.reidaboutsex.com

Reid Mihalko offers classes in L.A. on everything from overcoming jealousy in a relationship to the best way to negotiate a threesome with your lover. Or you can hire him one-on-one for coaching sessions or sign-up for one of his sex education field trips where he'll take you on a sex toy store tour to "Take a Sex Educator To Lunch Day." He has a lot to offer so visit his website to learn more.

THE SINGLE GIRL
www.thesinglegirl.la

The Single Girl website is for the naughty girl in all of us. This website is dedicated to all things naughty. Whether you're single, in a relationship, living with someone or married, this website is for you. You can visit here to play naughty games with your lover to spice things up, take online sex classes, visit The Erotic Museum to learn about sex in history—and much more. You'll also learn how to tap into your inner naughty self by feeling more sexual and gorgeous in and out of the bedroom.

NAUGHTY LIFESTYLE COACH
www.naughtylifestylecoach.com

Get one-on-one coaching from your Naughty Lifestyle Expert, Sienna Sinclaire. I offer coaching services for sex, relationships and dating. You can call, email or meet in person for our sessions. I can coach those who already have a great sex life but want to learn some new techniques to spice it up, or those who lack the confidence to meet someone new. I've been in the adult industry for over seven years and have a lot of hands-on experience that you can't learn in sex schools.

EMBODY TANTRA
www.embodytantra.com

If you're looking to not only increase your pleasure but also to expand your mind and stay rooted in the moment, look to tantra. Embody Tantra offers classes and one-on-one coaching for single women and couples and can help you unlock a lot of hidden desires and pleasures within you.

———— NAUGHTY BY DAY ————

FREDDY AND EDDY
www.freddyandeddy.com

Want to know the best way to have sex in a car? Or which lubes are the best for anal play? This website is full of sex-education advice, it just depends on what you're interested in learning. They offer free podcasts on all kinds of sexual topics and reviews on the best sex toys and adult websites.

FETISH CLASSES

AVATAR L.A.
www.avatarla.org

Avatar L.A. was formed in the early 1980s as an organization to provide safe education to gay men interested in the BDSM lifestyle. They now offer education for anyone—regardless of sex, race, religion or sexual preference. You can attend one of their demonstrations, play parties or hands-on classes where they cover everything from basics such as "Bondage 101" to more advance BDSM scenes.

PLEASURE CHEST
7733 Santa Monica Blvd., West Hollywood
323.650.1022
www.thepleasurechest.com

The Pleasure Chest also offers fetish classes among their many other sex-education seminars and they are all FREE. You can get your feet wet if you're new to fetish play by taking their spanking, flogging, watersports or fisting classes. Just check their schedule or call ahead to see what's being offered.

NAUGHTY BY DAY

BDSM CLASSES
www.bdsmclasses.com

This is an extensive site with classes in all levels of the BDSM lifestyle. They offer discussions on various topics, including sexuality, alternative relationships choices and sado-masochistic behaviors. You can find information here on being a novice slave, mastering dominance and even having a master-servant relationship over long distances. There is so much to learn if you're interested in the BDSM lifestyle or if you're already an expert.

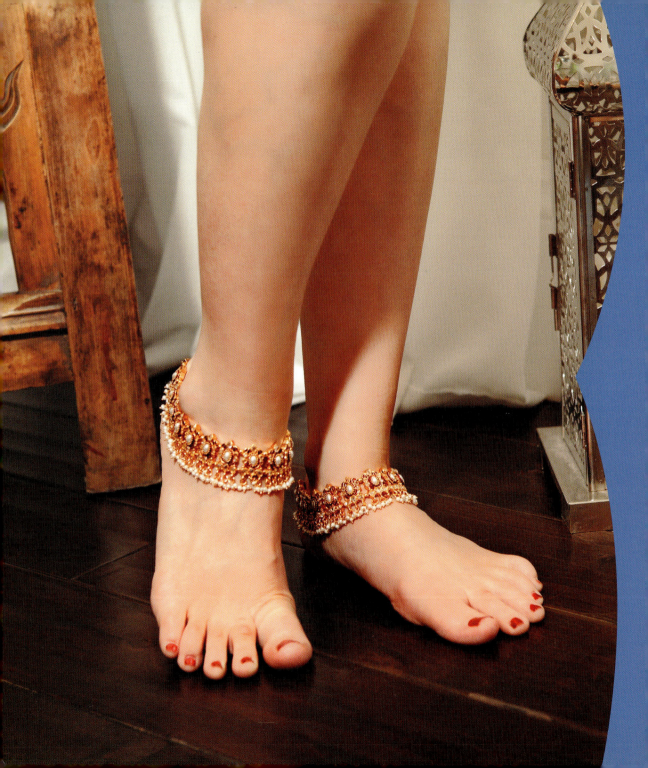

SEXY DANCE CLASSES

Many people shy away from the dance floor because they're afraid of looking foolish. If you want to be a better dancer, look into dance classes. You don't have to be an expert dancer, just learn the basic dance steps and you'll look like a professional on the dance floor. There are many sexy styles of dance for everyone—from pole to burlesque to flamenco. You can find training for any kind of dance style you can think of, and many you likely don't even know about yet. If you still have some stage fright after taking a dance course, you can always give your lover a private dance show. You can also encourage them to join you and find a new way to explore each other's body and provide a romantic spark to your relationship. Plus, dancing is a great way to get in shape and feel sexy about yourself. You've seen "Dancing With The Stars" and how amazing their bodies look after they take up dancing, so just think about how amazing you'll look along with your new-found confidence.

POLE DANCING & STRIPTEASE CLASSES

S FACTOR
5225 Wilshire Blvd., Suite B, Los Angeles
323.965.9685
www.sfactor.com

Taught by well-known fitness and dance author Sheila Kelley, who was featured on the Oprah Winfrey Show. You can learn her S-Factor workout by taking a class (introductory or private) that combines ballet, yoga and striptease. Or you can take her popular Eight-Week Series that combines the S-Factor workout with dance, striptease and pole work. If you can't make it to L.A. or if you want to try pole dancing on your own at home, then you can purchase the S-Factor DVD Series from her website.

ALLURE DANCE & FITNESS STUDIO
5996 W. Pico Blvd., West L.A.
310.343.9757
www.poledanceallure.com

They offer classes for "pole virgins" and even offer various fitness classes throughout the week. Or you can host your own pole party with your girlfriends by choosing from their Allure Pole or Sensual Seduction Party package. They even offer a FREE Friday night pole instruction and chair dance class at the J Spot Comedy Club. Visit their website for more details on the free class and how to sign up.

---- NAUGHTY BY DAY ----

EVOLVE DANCE STUDIO
5872 Pico Blvd., Suite A, West L.A.
323.230.9605
www.evolverevolutionstudios.com

You can go beyond the pole here with aerial hoop classes, yoga and "Stiletto Fit" classes to help improve your strut in your best high heels. For a more personalized program or for those who may be a bit shy at first, they offer private classes where a professional trainer will cater to your individual needs.

LUSCIOUS MAVEN
11101 Ventura Blvd., Studio City
310.962.5783
www.lusciousmaven.com

The delectable Heather West has a studio that offers weekly pole-dance classes, pole parties, workshops, teacher training and private pole-dance lessons. They also teach burlesque, belly dance, aerial arts, fire dance, yoga, acrobatics and more. Visit her website for more details.

NAUGHTY GIRL'S GUIDE TO LOS ANGELES

HEART & POLE DANCE AND FITNESS
528 Pacific Coast Hwy., Hermosa Beach
310.937.7653
www.heartandpole.com

Believing there's a dancer in every woman, this studio offers not only pole dancing, but Girlie Burlesque, Bikini Body, Stilletease and Sensual Yoga classes. You can take one of their drop-in classes or six-week workshops, or host a private party with your girlfriends.

NAUGHTY BY DAY

THE SECRET POLE DANCE STUDIO
5225 Wilshire Blvd. Suite B, Los Angeles
323.965.9685
www.thesecretpoleparties.com

This studio prides itself on being a fun learning environment and catering to women of all sizes. Plus you don't have to share a pole with anyone either as they keep their class sizes small. They offer three levels to pole dancing, so you can come in as a beginner and leave an expert. After you've mastered the pole you can take their "Exotic Movement" class by learning sexy floor moves.

FROM MIND TO BODY
817 N. Highland Ave., Hollywood
888.632.2236
www.frommindtobody.com

You can learn pole tricks, chair dance and floor work at this Hollywood studio by signing up for one of their many sexy classes. They also offer party packages and will even come to your hotel to teach you pole lessons.

ISABELLE'S DANCE ACADEMY
1334 Lincoln Blvd., 2nd Floor, Santa Monica
310.392.3493
www.isabellesalsa.com

An impressive studio with an equally impressive lineup of pole and lap-dancing classes. They keep their class sizes to a minimum so that everyone has their own pole. If you're new to pole dancing, then take their four-week pole dancing class (new classes starting weekly).

POLISTIC POLE DANCE & SEXY PILATES
12526 Ventura Blvd., Studio City
818.769.4364
www.polistic.com

Set in a beautiful studio and open to women of all shapes, they make sure you're always comfortable with your progress. You can choose between their introduction to pole dance, sexy pilates or pole trix class. Also, every month they offer different workshops—including burlesque, lap dancing and Bikini Boot Camp—so make sure to check out their website for updates.

MOON DANCE STUDIOS
705-A Coronada Ave., Long Beach
562.552.2251
www.moondancestudio.net

They not only offer pole dancing, but also hula, burlesque and salsa dancing. You can choose from their Burlesque Lapdance Striptease, Lapdance, Pole & Striptease or Cardio Strip classes. Their classes are offered weekly and the dates change monthly so check their website for a current schedule.

BESPUN
5176 Santa Monica Blvd., Hollywood
323.665.5856
www.bespun.com

They specialize in pole dancing and can take you from the basics all the way to advance with their many pole dancing classes. They even offer private one-on-one sessions, parties with your girlfriends, and workshops for beginners to intermediate levels. If you can't make it to L.A., or you're a bit shy, purchase one of their DVD's to see if pole dancing is for you.

APHRODITE POLE DANCE FITNESS STUDIO
630 N La Cienega Blvd., West Hollywood
323.272.3179
www.aphroditesnp.com

This studio emphasizes getting in touch with your libido and slowing down to appreciate not only your body but also the moment. Once you've mastered pole dancing with their six-week Master Class you can take part in their annual Halloween show where all students will work on the choreography.

BURLESQUE CLASSES

LUSCIOUS MAVEN
11101 Ventura Blvd., Studio City
310.962.5783
www.lusciousmaven.com

The scrumptious Ali Kat can teach you to unleash your inner striptease girl at Heather West's studio in Studio City. Ali offers a two-hour intensive workshop for beginners and two five-week workshops for those who want to work on their choreography (for beginner or advanced students). Visit their website for updated classes, as they are offered by the month.

ALL STAR BURLESQUE CLASSES
818.404.9459
www.learnburlesque.net

Penny Starr Jr. teaches fabulous monthly burlesque classes, which you can find on her website. Every month is different so make sure to check out her calendar. You can learn how to take it off, how to perform solo, how to fan dance and much more. Or you can take private lessons if you want to focus on something more specific.

NAUGHTY BY DAY

DK DANCE STUDIO
5505 Laurel Canyon Blvd., Valley Village
818.980.4635
www.dkdancefactory.com

Every Tuesday they offer "Girlesque Burlesque." This is a fun and girly class for those looking for a different kind of workout. It's a mix of burlesque, musical theatre and jazz that will get your heart pumping and hips shaking. You'll leave the class feeling sexy and ready to show off your new moves to your lover.

SCHOOL OF BURLESQUE
www.kittendeville.net

Classes are taught by the world-famous Kitten de Ville, who offers a School of Burlesque on her website. This class is for those who are interested in trying out burlesque or who want to add some new moves to their routine. It's a six-week workshop where you'll get the chance to perform in front of an audience at the end of the course. You can also hire her one-on-one to learn burlesque on your own or for private parties.

BELLY DANCE CLASSES

NILE DANCE
122 W. Garvey Ave., Monterey Park
213.458.2592
www.niledance.com

Nile Dance is a community for belly dancers that combines Egyptian and Oriental dances. Women of all ages and shapes are welcome. Classes are structured to help students get fit, learn rhythm and absorb the sensual aspects of the dance. Students learn at their own pace in group or private classes, solo and/or group performances, and special workshops.

PRINCESS FARHANA
www.princessfarhana.com

The world-famous Princess Farhana has performed all over the world. She was named "Favorite Oriental Dancer 2006 and 2008" by Zaghareet Magazine. She has danced for celebrities and dignitaries such as Hilary Clinton, the Saudi Arabian royal family and the Rolling Stones. She teaches burlesque and other types of dance all over the world. Her belly dance fundamentals will also teach you veil work and finger cymbals. Check her calendar, as classes are limited.

NAUGHTY BY DAY

LUMINA ACADEMY
1052 North Allen Ave., Pasadena
626.296.2812
www.luminaacademy.com

Lumina Academy is among the best places in L.A. County to learn dances from around the world. It offers group and private lessons for children and adults. Course offerings include Argentine tango, belly dancing, ballet, Bollywood style, Brazilian samba, break dancing, flamenco, salsa and many more. They have no more than twelve students per class here, so you can get a lot of individual attention. They also have a salsa party every second Friday (it's only five dollars to get in).

ANISA'S SCHOOL OF DANCE
14252 Ventura Blvd., Sherman Oaks
818.908.8008
www.anisadance.com

Anisa's offers a wide variety of dance and fitness classes taught by professional instructors. You can have a fun girls' night out learning dances from Spain, Argentina, the Middle East

PRINCESS FARHANA

and India. Ballet, jazz, modern, hip-hop, tap and other dance classes are available for all ages. They also offer many exercise and fitness classes in a "non-gym" atmosphere. After you learn the dance arts, you can join Anisa on a dance tour of Egypt or Turkey.

BELLY TWINS
310.285.2255
www.bellytwins.com

The gorgeous Belly Twins—Neena and Veena—have been featured as dancers, choreographers and actresses on hundreds of stages, films, TV shows, commercials and music videos worldwide. They teach not only Bollywood, bhangra and belly dance, but also sword and veil dances. They also have created a lot of belly-dance fitness products, and have produced over fifteen instructional and fitness videos, some of which had long runs on the Billboard Top Ten charts. Fitness magazine named some of their videos as the "Top Ten Videos of the Year."

MIDDLE EASTERN DANCER
310.922.4362
www.middleeasterndancer.com

Tamra-henna is an internationally acclaimed performer, choreographer and master instructor of Middle Eastern dance and has delighted audiences since 1991. Students in her weekly class include many superstars of belly dance. All of her classes are based on the Egyptian style of raqs sharqi—the "mother of all belly-dance styles." Tamra-henna also teaches students the music and proper technique so they have a better understanding of the art.

OCEANA DANCE
323.394.2300
www.oceanadance.com

Oceana has been teaching dynamic belly dance art for the last eight years in Egyptian and American cabaret styles. She's also a snake dancer and a featured dancer at the Moroccan restaurant Dar Maghreb in Hollywood. Oceana has performed for Victoria Beckham, Charlise Theron and Kate Beckinsale. She loves teaching the healing and empowering parts of the art. She also teaches a fun "Bellydance Burn" class that focuses on the fitness aspects of the art.

SHA'WAZA BELLY DANCE
2620 E. Walnut St., Pasadena
435.632.6495
www.shawazabellydance.com

Sha'Waza Belly Dance not only teaches dance but also "moving meditation" to encourage their students to deal with stress and to appreciate life and being a woman. They love teaching groups and have many classes and options for all ages, shapes and levels of skill. They host girls'-night-out events and also teach tribal drumming, strings and wind instruments. Their style is known as American Tribal Style and is mostly improvised, so each performance is different.

ADAM BASMA
1551 S. La Cienega Blvd., West L.A.
323.934.9493
www.adambasma.com

Adam Basma teaches Middle Eastern dance to students of all levels and has been bringing dance arts to the U.S. from Egypt, Syria, Algeria, Lebanon, Palestine, Jordan, the Arabian Gulf and Morocco since 1980. His classes on Sunday are open to everyone and he has one-on-one private sessions for those who perform on stage. He has world-renowned musicians at his studio, so the music there is top-notch. They claim to be "the best Middle Eastern dancing school in the USA."

MESMERA
323.669.0333
www.mesmera.com

Mesmera has been featured in *Time, InStyle* and *L.A. Weekly* and has taught and performed for over two decades. She's an inspiring performer and instructor who encourages freedom of movement in her dance classes. She offers classes and videos and even private video training if you can't make it to L.A. She also teaches Mother-Daughter classes and offers travel retreats to Spain every year. To learn more about her retreats, visit her website.

AISHA-ALI
3270 Kelton Ave., Los Angeles
310.474.4867
www.aisha-ali.com

Aisha Ali is belly-dancing legend. She has taught, studied, written about and performed dances from the Middle East and Asia since the 1970s. She even directed the North African performers at the Los Angeles Olympics opening ceremony in 1984. Aisha gives lectures and demonstrations at UCLA and Cornell, and conducts workshops and master classes all over the world. You cannot ask for a more knowledgeable instructor—and she only charges fifteen dollars for a class!

ROUHI DANCE STUDIO
19320 Ventura Blvd., Tarzana
818.609.9991
www.rouhidancestudio.com

This dance studio offers a wide variety of classes. You can learn belly dance, salsa, tango, hip-hop or ballroom dance. They feature a "Dance Open House" where you can try out a lesson for free. No prior experience is needed and their classes give you a great workout. You can take belly-dance classes as a fitness program, or go deeper to learn the intricate aspects of the art.

DANCE GARDEN
3407 Glendale Blvd., Los Angeles
323.660.4556
www.dancegardenla.com

Jenna and Zahra Zuhair founded Dance Garden in 2007 and have a clientele that includes National Geographic Television and The Boot dating show. Dance Garden teaches beginners to advanced practitioners everything from belly dancing to Zumba. They even offer a belly-dancing boot camp! With instructors that are all easy on the eyes, Dance Garden also provides space for rehearsals, photo shoots and filming.

DANCING RAHANA
310.612.7622
www.dancingrahana.com

Rahana believes that "the expression of passion is just as important as the movement of dance." She's the Director of Bella Oasis Dance Company (formally Troupe Bahiya) and is highly skilled in traditional belly dance, in ballet and in the American Cabaret–style of belly dance. She can take you from the basics all the way to being a full-fledged performer. But visit her website first, as she teaches in many different locations around L.A.

SALSA CLASSES

LATIN DANCE
310.869.8313
www.latindance.com

The lovely Josie Neglia teaches everything from salsa to hip hop and welcomes students of all ages and sizes. She offers group lessons in L.A., Long Beach and West L.A., or you can take private lessons. If you can't make it to L.A., then you can order her instructional DVDs or download her salsa classes online—where you can learn quick sexy moves before heading out on the town.

3RD STREET DANCE
8558 W. 3rd St., Los Angeles
310.275.4683
www.3rdstreetdance.com

Classes are ongoing here, so you can start anytime. No partner is required and they offer three beginners salsa classes per week. You may show up as often as you like. They also have a "Salsa Blast" workout class and a "Ladies Salsa Styling Workshop" to help you focus on the sexier sides of the art. They even offer tango, ballroom and swing classes, so make sure to check out their website for a list of all their wonderful classes.

BALLROOM DANCE ACADEMY
817 N. Highland Ave., Hollywood
323.467.0825
www.ballroomdanceacademy.com

They not only offer salsa courses, but also all the major ballroom and Latin dances. You can sign-up for their "Intro. Package to Salsa," which includes two private sessions plus enrollment into the the four-week Salsa Series. They even offer master ballroom classes to take you to a competitive level. They let you learn at your own pace and stress high-quality instruction in a fun environment. They even throw Salsa Night parties every Tuesday, where you can practice your dance moves with other students.

THE SALSA BOX STUDIOS
560 S. Main St., Downtown L.A.
323.972.1831
www.thesalsaboxstudios.com

Instructor Lisa Feliciano has been dancing Salsa since she was a child and is trained in ballet, jazz, modern, Afro-Cuban, tap, swing and tango. This studio offers a lot of personal attention and keeps a low student-to-instructor ratio. They know that big, impersonal classes can be intimidating to someone without any dance training, so don't worry if you've never tried salsa before. They also offer private salsa dance instruction if you're really shy. They even offer "Practice Mixers" where you can dance with other students.

LEARN SALSA
4200 Lankershim Blvd., N. Hollywood
213.761.7900
www.learnsalsa.com

These folks have famous salsa boot camps that can teach you to salsa in six hours or less! It's a great alternative to the gym and gives you a solid cardio workout. They claim you'll burn 1,500 calories at Salsa Boot Camp. They have a constant rotation of partners, so you'll dance with everyone (40 to 50 people!) of the opposite sex. It could even be a fun, sexy way to meet someone special. Plus they have two locations: North Hollywood and Los Angeles.

L.A. DANCE EXPERIENCE
1941 Westwood Blvd., Westwood
310.475.1878
www.ladanceexperience.com

Apart from ballroom and tango classes, L.A. Dance Experience offers three levels of salsa classes here that can take you from novice to "the one to be seen with at any Salsa dance." They keep the classes balanced by having an equal number of men and women in the classes and rotate partners so you'll be certain to dance with that hot guy you saw when you first walked into the studio. They even offer private lessons, dance parties and workshops.

TAHITIAN AND HULA DANCE CLASSES

HALAU HULA A KAWIKA LAUA 'O LEINANI
Diamond Bar
909.396.4775
www.kawikaleinani.com

This studio teaches both ancient hula ("Kahiko") and modern hula ("Auana"). You'll begin each class by learning the basics, along with how to greet each other in Hawaiian language.

ISLAND PRIDE ENTERTAINMENT
562.434.4125
www.islandprideentertainment.webs.com

You can learn not only hula, Polynesian and Tahitian dance here, but also fire and knife dancing. Once you've perfected your hula moves you can move to the next level by performing on stage with their group or solo.

PACIFIC ISLAND DANCERS
3727 Honeysuckle Dr., Chino Hills
909.606.2682
www.pacificislanddancers.com

They offer classes for Hawaiian, Tahitian, Maori, Philippine Islands and Samoan dance. Hula basics and advanced techniques are taught here, along with drumming lessons, dance workshops and private classes.

TE VARUA ORI
6122 Orangethorpe Ave., Suite 110, Buena Park
714.761.1883
www.tevaruaori.com

Their class sessions are offered four times a year. Check their website for dates, as classes are not ongoing. All classes start off at beginner level; intermediate ones are by invitation only.

OTHER SEXY CLASSES

FLAMENCO CLASSES

ROCIO PONCE
1866 E. 1st St., Downtown L.A.
323.333.7067
www.rocioponce.com

Whether you're just looking to have fun and learn the basics or become an expert, they offer basic classes to intensive programs. Also, make sure to check out their website for their workshops, as they are constantly offering different ones each month.

THE ARTE FLAMENCO DANCE THEATRE
230 W. Main St., Alhambra
626.458.1234
www.clarita-arteflamenco.com

They offer three levels of flamenco classes here, as well as many types of dance—from ballet to hip hop. For your dance classes or performances you can buy hard-to-find flamenco skirts, shoes and accessories at their store, along with educational materials that can help you perfect your dancing.

TANGO CLASSES

MAKELA TANGO
12121 W. Pico Blvd., Suite 2C, Los Angeles
310.740.2007
www.makelatango.com

They offer affordable semi-private classes, private coaching and even ladies-only classes. Once you've learned your basic tango steps you can head to Buenos Aires with Makela Tango to practice your moves. Registration is limited, so visit the website for more details.

TANGO ACADEMY OF PASADENA
57 Palmetto Dr., Pasadena
626.584.0774
www.tangoacademypasadena.com

Apart from offering three levels of tango classes, they also organize "tango tours" of Buenos Aires. You can attend these tours with or without previous tango experience. On the two-week tours you'll visit different tango clubs, explore the city and receive Tango lessons.

AERIAL CLASSES

THE AERIAL CLASSROOM
Van Nuys
866.529.8085
www.theaerialclassroom.com

Learn to fly on silk, hoops, the trapeze and more. The Aerial Classroom even offers circus training—from tight rope to contortion classes—for those interested in joining the circus. Check their website to see when the classes are being offered. You can also sign up for private lessons.

CIRQUE SCHOOL
5640 1/2 Hollywood Blvd., Los Angeles
323.333.7067
www.cirqueschoolla.com

Cirque School is "for anybody with any body." They'll teach you the basics and help you develop your own aerial act and more. Or, if you're just looking for something different from the gym, they offer an "Aerial Fitness & Conditioning" class that will strengthen the whole body. They have so much to offer, including interesting workshops, so make sure to visit their website.

FIRE CLASS

FIRE GROOVE
1866 E. 1st St., Downtown L.A.
800.755.6423
www.firegroove.com

Learn how to play with fire and create an exotic performance for your lover. You can also learn to eat fire and paint your body with it. If you'd rather stay away from the flames, they also teach hoop dancing. They offer tons of sexy classes, along with DVDs to learn how to dance with fire.

BOLLYWOOD CLASS

NDM BOLLYWOOD DANCE STUDIO
17711 S. Pioneer Blvd., Artesia
323.333.7067
www.ndmdance.com

This school specializes in dancing styles from Bollywood. They teach Bhangra, Bollywood dancing, Folk, Indian-influenced hip-hop and bride-and-groom dances. They have locations in Northridge, Irvine, Artesia and San Diego. Visit their website for locations and schedules.

SEXY FITNESS

If you're looking to stay on your workout schedule while you're in L.A., why not make your workout a sexy one? L.A. has plenty of options for workouts that are designed to make you sweat one way so you'll be hyped up to sweat the other way.

SEXY TRAINER

JOSHUA LOVE
www.kinemafitness.com

He trains celebrities, Playboy models and porn stars, just to name a few. You can work out with him at the sexy Viceroy hotel (check my hotel list) in their gym, at the nearby beach or one-on-one at your home or hotel. He can help you customize any fitness routine to fit your needs to make sure you stay in shape while on vacation.

SEXY GYM

EQUINOX
210 Santa Monica Blvd., Santa Monica
310.593.8888
www.equinox.com

My vote for sexiest gym in L.A. is the Equinox in Santa Monica. It was even voted "Best Gym in America" by *Fitness* magazine. Lots of celebrities work out here, along with sexy guys all hours of the day. It has four floors, making it more private for those who like a more intimate workout. Plus they have four studios for their workout classes, along with a pilates studio that is separate from the gym. They offer tons of weekly workout classes, along with "Boom Boom Burlesque" so that you won't get bored. They also have a nice spa, located on the fourth floor, along with a steam room for relaxing your muscles after your workout.

SEXY FITNESS CLASSES

CRUNCH FITNESS
www.crunch.com

If you stay near a Crunch Fitness center you can get in on sexy fitness classes such as Strip Bar, Turning Tricks and Pole Dancing. Or, if you don't feel comfortable in front of others, you can still take these classes by signing up for their private sessions. You pick the class and they'll customize it to fit your needs.

HOST A NAUGHTY PARTY

Whether you live in L.A. or want to have a sexy getaway with your girlfriends or bachelorette party, plan a sexy party that you'll all remember and talk about for years to come. On the next few pages are different ideas to help you plan your naughty party. Begin by choosing one, two or all the options listed to make your party the naughtiest.

FIRE AND AERIAL DANCERS

ZEN ARTS
310.259.7642
www.zenartsla.com

They offer a variety of sexy dancers (including fire, go-go, belly, burlesque, samba and capoeira) for your next event. You can even hire contortionists, aerialists, acrobats, hoopers, live muralists, snake charmers, stilt walkers, cirque characters and DJs.

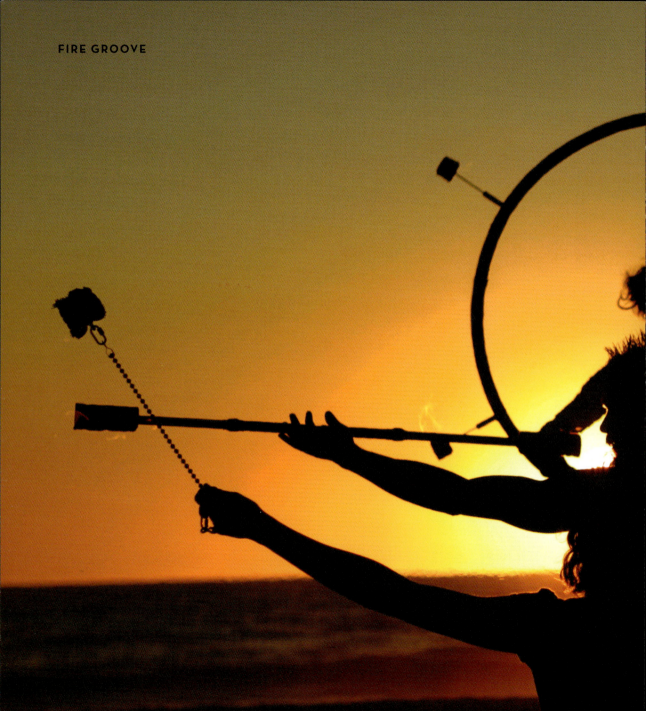

FIRE GROOVE
800.755.6423

www.firegroove.com

They have a lot of options for different themed events, making it hard to pick your favorite one. Your job is to choose what type of show you're looking for along with the theme. Sound easy? Just wait till you take a look at their website. They offer pole dancers, aerialists, fire dancers, glow performers, hoopers, go-go dancers . . . and the list goes on and on. You can choose between themes that include tribal, Moulin rouge, carnival, golden goddess party and more.

STRIPPERS

CA EXOTIC DANCERS
888.880.7675

www.caexoticdancers.com

Let them provide the entertainment for your next event—all you need to do is sit back and enjoy the show. You can hire sexy men to serve at your event, along with hiring a few more for a sexy strip show. They offer both male and female performers.

BURLESQUE PERFORMERS

ALL-STAR BURLESQUE CLASSES
818.404.9459
www.learnburlesque.net

Penny Starr Jr. will come to your party and teach you and your girlfriends to shake your groove things. You can even buy pasties as party favors. You can create your own party by contacting Penny or join one of her weekly classes with your girlfriends.

POLE- AND LAP-DANCING PARTIES

ISABELLA'S DANCE ACADEMY
310.392.3493
www.isabellesalsa.com

You and your girlfriends can choose between lap, pole or striptease dance-class parties. When you show up to her studio you'll get the chance to "dress up" in your own naughty outfits while sipping on wine to relax and loosen up for an afternoon of naughty fun with your girlfriends.

ALLURE DANCE & FITNESS STUDIO
5996 W. Pico Blvd., West L.A.
310.343.9757
www.poledanceallure.com

They offer good rates for parties that feature sexy performers and lessons for you and your girlfriends. You can choose between the Allure Pole or Sensual Seduction Party and you can pay a little extra to have a professional photographer capture all your naughty moments on film. Also, if you don't want the hassle of planning a party you can attend their "Free J Spot Pole Party" every Friday with your girlfriends. Visit their website for more details.

SEX TOY PARTIES

EROTIC MAINSTREAM
877.265.7233
www.eroticmainstream.net

They guarantee a night or afternoon full of fun where you will get to sample, touch and taste products—along with becoming educated about lubricants, vibrators and sex toys. Plus, as a hostess you will get a free gift and tons of discounts!

SWEET SEDUCTIONZ
www.sweetseductionz.net

They can bring all sorts of naughty toys and treats to your bachelorette party or "naughty girl" party. They offer several different packages starting at $50. You can customize your party and make it even naughtier by adding a photographer, exotic dancers, professional masseuse and pole-dancing lessons.

FOR YOUR PLEASURE
562.618.6303
www.foryourpleasure.net/lizdube

Contact Liz Dube for "your ultimate girl's night in!" She offers romance, pole- and lap-dancing parties, along with bedroom accessories for greater passion. She'll get everything you need for your naughty party—you just show up with your girlfriends and get ready for a night of fun and laughter.

PRIVATE SEX PARTIES

JAMYE WAXMAN
www.jamyewaxman.com

You can hire Jamye to come to your house or anywhere else to hold private workshops for your friends. Her workshops are usually ninety minutes and can be tailored to fit your specific needs. She covers topics on ways to talk to your lover, learning more about sex toys and anatomy, techniques for better sex and much more.

NAUGHTY BY DAY

LOVEOLOGY UNIVERSITY
www.loveologyuniversity.com

Dr. Ava offers private seminars on finding love, enriching relationships, creating romance, enhancing intimacy and expanding sexuality for a more fulfilling life. There's not much that she doesn't cover, so check out her website for a list of topics. You can even take your own online sex classes by yourself, with your partner or girlfriends.

NUDE BEACHES

One thing you need to know is that there are no nude beaches in L.A. according to Los Angeles County ordinance # 17.12.360. "No person shall appear, bathe, sunbathe, walk, change clothes, disrobe or be on any beach in such manner that the genitals, vulva, pubis, pubic symphysis, pubic hair, buttocks, natal cleft, perineum, anus, anal region or pubic hair region of any person, or any portion of the breast at or below the upper edge of the areola thereof of any female person, is exposed to public view, except in those portions of a comfort station, if any, expressly set aside for such purpose."

That being said, you need to know where to go so you won't be fined. There are two beaches in L.A. County where people tend to get nude and no one seems to mind, but if you're up for a little drive you can sunbathe nude and avoid the cops (unless you're like me and wouldn't mind them stopping by).

A good nude or topless beach has some basic unwritten rules. No gawking, no groping, no unsolicited advances. Everyone's expected to have an open mind, to accept all ages of adults and all body types and to respect boundaries. Is there sex on nude beaches? Sure, but it is not as common as many think. It's easy to think an orgy could break out at any moment if you watch enough naughty movies, but don't hold your breath waiting for it. Most people are there for an "all-over tan" and a little sexy excitement. Now, if you meet a fun group of people and have enough room in your hotel . . . .

LOS ANGELES COUNTY BEACHES

ABALONE COVE

This beach in Rancho Palos Verdes is one of the few in L.A. County where people sometimes get naked. The Abalone Cove Shoreline Park is beautiful. It even contains a state ecological preserve. You can't barbecue there or bring your dog, but you probably weren't planning on doing either if you'd planned on sunbathing in the buff. It's five dollars to park there and it's a short walk to the beach. The area is full of neat things to explore.

POINT DUME

This is another gorgeous park in L.A. County (Malibu, to be precise) where you can sometimes tan topless. It's an amazing place. You can see whales from here during the winter months. On clear days the views are breathtaking—you can see Santa Monica Bay, Catalina Island, the Malibu coast and the Santa Monica Mountains. A lot of movies and TV shows are filmed here, so who knows whom you might see in the buff?

BEACHES OUTSIDE OF LOS ANGELES COUNTY

GAVIOTA BEACH

This beach is in Gaviota State Park in Santa Barbara County and next to the Los Padres National Forest. The beach has a campground with sites for RV and tent camping, so you can have a private place for frisky fun with someone you meet on the beach. The beach can be windy, especially in the spring, so bear that in mind when you go. There are high cliffs here that keep gawkers at a minimum. You can watch whales there sometimes. Make sure to avoid the poison oak!

MORE MESA BEACH

This white sand beach in Santa Barbara County is popular and full of different activities from volleyball to nude sunbathing. The nude section of the beach is to the north (to the right of the trail), so stay there if you want to avoid the park rangers. A lot of people go there so you'll be able to see a lot of nice bodies, even if you don't go to the nude-sunbathing section. It's about a mile walk to the beach from the parking area, so wear some comfy shoes.

RINCON BEACH

This beach in Santa Barbara is a popular surfing spot. The sand can disappear at high tide, so make sure to appropriately time your visit. There are some nice spots to watch the surfers or see the Channel Islands on a good day. Surfing is the main attraction here, so bring a good book if watching buff and sexy surfers isn't your thing—although I don't know why that would be the case.

SUMMERLAND BEACH

Another Santa Barbara beach (south of town), this used to be one of the most popular beaches for nude sunbathing. There have been crackdowns in recent years, so be careful when you decide to get naked. The park rangers scan the area and often issue tickets for public nudity. It's just off Highway 101, so it's easy to find.

SAN ONOFRE

This state park is between L.A. and San Diego and it includes an amazing 3,000-acre beach. It's world-famous for its surfing and has even hosted the world tandem surfing championships. San Onofre Beach is the closest clothing-optional beach to L.A. and Orange County. It's been the subject of some fights in court for citations issued to nude sunbathers found near the volleyball courts. Some of the park rangers watch sunbathers from high on the cliffs to see if you're nude, but you can find hundreds of nude sunbathers here on a hot day.

DEANZA SPRINGS RESORT
This is a nudist camp in Jacumba in San Diego County. It's in the high desert mountains and has rental suites, RV sites and tent camping. It has tons of amenities—hot tubs, clubhouse, fitness center, heated pools, volleyball courts and more. The pools and hot tubs have a strict "No clothes allowed" policy!

BLACKS BEACH
The nude sunbathers at this San Diego beach hold a beach picnic every Sunday during the summer. The park rangers have moved most of the nude sunbathing to a marked area (look for the signs on the cliffs) that's actually Torrey Pines State Beach. It's one of the largest clothing optional beaches in the country (over two miles long) and wildly popular. It's not far from the San Diego campus of the University of California, so you might see a lot of yummy coed eye candy. Most of the nudists sunbathe north of the Glider Port Trail, so drift that way once you arrive.

Naughty Shopping

BEAUTY

Hollywood has always been obsessed with beauty. Filmmakers quickly figured out that putting beautiful people on screen was another good way to bring people into theatres. Moviegoers fantasized about being as glamorous as Marilyn Monroe or as dashing as William Powell. Men wanted to see all of Jane Russell's assets. Women wanted to look like Jane Russell to bring their husbands home from work every day.

Hollywood magazines quickly catered to the desire for everyday Americans to look like their movie idols. Women were, and still are, especially keen to learn all the Hollywood beauty secrets.

Max Factor catered to the movie stars in the very beginning (as early as 1914). The company knew that the popularity of films worldwide would also take their products international. They became the cosmetics company for many Hollywood starlets and made special products for Jean Harlow, Claudette Colbert, Clara Bow, Rudolph Valentino and many others. You can view their vintage beauty products at The Hollywood Museum at the old Max Factor Building.

Hollywood's obsession with beauty has grown to an extreme—now often involving surgery and unhealthy diets. I'm here to show you how to do it all-natural without surgery or downtime from painful treatments. Trust me: you can look as beautiful as any actress on the red carpet without going under the knife.

SEXY HAIR

KEN PAVES HAIR SALON
409 N. Robertson Blvd., Beverly Hills
310.205.0087
www.kenpaves.com

Some of the sexiest women alive get their hair done here. Megan Fox, Jessica Simpson and Desperate Housewives' hottie Eva Longoria come here to look great. At Ken Paves Salon they love to make women look amazing and feel good, which is why I keep going back. They have many stylists on hand who each specialize in something different—from color, cutting, hair extensions, blowouts to Brazilian Keratin treatments.

NAUGHTY SHOPPING

LASER HAIR REMOVAL

SKIN REMEDIES
1828 Broadway, Suite B, Santa Monica
310.453.6474
www.skinremedies.com

Get sexy legs and a soft coochie with laser hair removal from Carrie Elder. After about six treatments you'll no longer have to worry about shaving, stubble or razor burn. She works on many big names in the adult industry, including Jesse Jane and me. She uses a lot of minimally invasive methods and her anti-aging treatments are done without surgery.

ANAL BLEACHING

PINK CHEEKS
14562 Ventura Blvd., Sherman Oaks
818.906.8225
www.pinkcheeks.com

This used to be a bit of a taboo subject, but it's become more mainstream in the last few years due to porn stars. It's easy to do, you just have to apply bleaching crème every night. Everyone responds to the treatment at a different pace, so don't worry if you don't see results right away. If you can't make it to L.A. or if you're shy about going in, you can always order the crème by calling them.

SEXY MAKEOVER

NIKKI STAR
951.522.6924
www.nikkistarmakeup.com

Nikki Star is the makeup artist to some of the hottest stars in L.A. Contact her to come to your hotel or home for a personal makeover, including your hair. You can hire her one-on-one for makeovers, private parties with your girlfriends or private makeup classes so you can learn her techniques on your own.

ORGANIC SPRAY TAN

LAVISH TAN
1636 Abbot Kinney Blvd., Venice Beach
310.384.0010
www.lavishtan.com

Located in Venice, this place prides itself on using ninety-nine percent organic ingredients. Their treatments are brown sugar–based (not based on "orange-look" beta carotene), giving you a natural look that lasts one to two weeks. *Allure* magazine voted them "L.A.'s Best Organic Airbrushing Tanning Studio."

HISTORY OF LINGERIE IN LOS ANGELES

The preferred method of keeping time in Hollywood is by hourglass. If you don't believe me, just look at the shape of Hollywood starlets from past to present. For a while, the hourglass figure was considered too big for high fashion, but it's making a comeback and bringing in a new look to Hollywood glamour.

BRAS

Many famous classic actresses—including Mae West, Lana Turner, Marilyn Monroe and Jane Russell—became famous for their breasts. These women and their famous breasts brought about a new design in bras. Mae West was known as the sexiest woman of her day thanks to her frank attitude toward sex and because of her luscious curves. Lana Turner, the sweater girl, made falsies a big business for those who weren't well-endowed. And Marilyn Monroe was a size C, but her breasts looked bigger thanks to corsets specifically created to give her chest a boost.

The "bra that saved Hollywood" was worn by Jane Russell and thought of by Howard Hughes, who had hired Russell to star in his movie *The Outlaw*. The film was being savaged by critics and censors before its wide release and Hughes knew that the time and money he'd put into the film were on the verge of being wasted. One scene in *The Outlaw* required that Russell's breasts spill out of the top of her peasant blouse. However, the bras of 1943 covered too much cleavage. Hughes wanted Russell's bra to show her cleavage, but at the same time look as if she wasn't wearing a bra. It was a difficult task, but Hughes and his engineers created a bra that would do just that. With Russell's lovely breasts being displayed, Hughes flaunted the movie as a naughty controversial film—making it a box office smash and Russell's breasts the most famous in Hollywood. After the release of the movie, designs based on Jane Russell's bra became hot sellers.

During the 1950s another hot seller was the cone-shaped bra. The actresses who wore it were known as the "sweater girls." They included Diana Dors, Marilyn Monroe, Bridgette Bardot, Sophia Loren and Jayne Mansfield. Soon enough the cone-shaped bra was being mass-produced and bra companies were advertising to women across the nation that they could bring Hollywood glamour into their home and look like one of their favorite Hollywood starlets.

KNICKERS

The screen sirens of the 1940s made silk slips and French knickers popular because the Wills Hays Code banned starlets from wearing risqué lingerie. Therefore, French knickers were as raunchy as it got. Desperate to keep people coming to theatres, Hollywood kept movie-goers horny by putting their actresses in body-clinging silks and satins. Also, pin-up girls of the 1940s made French knickers popular by wearing them in provocative photo shoots.

LINGERIE STORES

Raunchy black lingerie became popular in Hollywood when Frederick Mellinger opened up his first lingerie store in the heart of Hollywood, Frederick's of Hollywood. Movie stars went to him for his sexy, European-style lingerie, Hollywood directors went to him for custom designs for their movies and women purchased from his catalogs in hopes of looking like their favorite Hollywood starlet. More than 50 years later, Frederick's of Hollywood is still famous and well-known today for their sexy, raunchy lingerie.

NAUGHTY GIRL'S GUIDE TO LOS ANGELES

HIGH-END LINGERIE STORES

TRASHY LINGERIE
402 N. La Cienega Blvd., West Hollywood
310.652.4543
www.trashy.com

Don't let the name fool you. They have a lot of nice collections here that can help you look like a naughty Stepford wife, schoolgirl, temptress or Bollywood queen. Their designs have appeared in tons of magazines, TV shows and movies. Lots of celebrities, models, Playboy bunnies and burlesque performers have shopped here, and many have appeared as models on their website, such as Dita Von Teese.

NAUGHTY SHOPPING

AGENT PROVOCATEUR
7961 Melrose Ave., L.A.
323.653.0229
www.agentprovocateur.com

This lingerie store is for the naughtier girl in us. They offer some of the sexiest lingerie and kinkiest toys, and are known for their naughty window displays. You won't find their pieces in other lingerie stores, as they design their own line of lingerie, nylons, shoes, accessories, dresses, swimwear and more. Plus, they have two locations in Los Angeles (Melrose Avenue and Rodeo Drive).

LA PERLA
433 N. Rodeo Dr., Beverly Hills
310.860.0561
www.laperla.com

This world-famous lingerie store offers gorgeous, elegant lingerie pieces for the more sophisticated woman. They even sell swimwear, loungewear, men's underwear and a bridal collection.

NAUGHTY GIRL'S GUIDE TO LOS ANGELES

FAIRE FROU FROU
13017 Ventura Blvd., Studio City
818.783.4970
www.fairefroufrou.com

This store is gorgeous and it has some of the sexiest lingerie. There is something here for everyone—from bunny slippers, pinup props, burlesque accessories to ooh-la-la lingerie. If you can't make it to the store, then visit the website to find the same lingerie carried in store (and more).

KIKI DE MONTPARNASSE
8280 Melrose Ave., West Hollywood
323.951.9545
www.kikidm.com

They have delicious, naughty lingerie selections here, along with high-quality sex toys to add to your night of pleasure. As soon as you walk

FAIRE FROU FROU

into their boutique you'll feel your inner naughty girl coming out immediately. This store is extremely sexy and sensual, and they have everything to make all your fantasies come to life.

UNDREST
8627 Melrose Ave., West Hollywood
310.360.0055
1136 Abbot Kinney Blvd., Venice Beach
310.314.1180

Their store is minimal and elegant, yet very sexy. Once you step inside you know you're surrounded by luxury. They offer sexy and unique pieces you won't find anywhere else—from lingerie to loungewear to swimwear. Their entire collection is made in-house in L.A.

FAIRE FROU FROU

PINK LILI

— NAUGHTY SHOPPING —

LINGERIE STORES

PINK LILI
1129 Montana Ave., Santa Monica
310.576.7100

Pink Lili is a very laid-back, casual lingerie store. It's sexy and cozy inside, which makes you want to shop there all day. Plus, they have an amazing outdoor patio where you can sit and chat with friends while shopping and trying on your sexy finds. The staff is really friendly and they sell all kinds of designer lingerie along with bathing suits.

PINK LILI

FREDERICK'S OF HOLLYWOOD
6751 Hollywood Blvd., Hollywood
323.957.5953
www.fredericks.com

Frederick Mellinger is the man who started it all with sexy black lingerie. His catalogs have made housewives and their husbands and lovers happy for decades. They offer lingerie—conservative, naughty or raunchy—for those with different tastes. Plus they offer affordable pieces for all budgets.

URSULA COSTUMES
2516 Wilshire Blvd., Santa Monica
310.582.8230
www.ursulascostumes.com

Come to this shop for Halloween costumes, fog machines, vampire fangs and anything else you need to play dress-up with your lover. You can find any kind of costume here, so you can be anyone you want. They cater to every big holiday in Los Angeles by carrying tons of costumes. If you're looking for a Renaissance costume for the yearly Renaissance Fair in L.A., then this is the place to go to rent or buy your outfit.

NAUGHTY SHOPPING

TRES JOLIE
350 S. Lake Ave. #114, Pasadena
626.795.5734
www.tresjolieintimates.com

You'll get one-on-one personalized service here from the owner Rose, who offers expert fitting and lots of attention to help you find exactly what you're looking for. They specialize in fine lingerie and sleepwear and new items arrive weekly, so you're sure to find something sexy.

BITTERSWEET BUTTERFLY
1406 Micheltorena St., Silver Lake
323.660.4303
www.bittersweetbutterfly.com

This is a very unique lingerie store because they offer a one-stop boutique for lingerie, flowers, sweets and jewelry. You'll find high-end lingerie ranging from French to New York designers, along with local jewelry designers and tasty body products. They even offer private lingerie and floral arrangement parties.

SEX & SPIKES

STILETTOS, HOLLYWOOD & SEX

There's no question that Hollywood constantly sells sex in films. In the golden age of Hollywood glamour, stars like Marilyn Monroe, Ava Gardner and Jane Russell became sex symbols and their high-heel shoes were put on full display for all to see on and off the screen. Stilettos became the sexy accessory that every woman wanted to have and that every man wanted their woman to wear.

Stiletto heels were first the ultimate fetish accessory for women (and some men!). Spike heels instantly told you who was boss. Bettie Page had hundreds of pairs and her photo shoots in naughty magazines were often viewed as fashion guides as much as they were fetish advice.

Stockings and stilettos turned schoolgirls into naughty mistresses and bored housewives into sex kittens. A woman wearing spike heels wasn't messing around. Stilettos became as important as a good haircut, or, in the case of Anita Ekberg in Fellini's *La Dolce Vita*, a champagne glass.

"Stars of the silver screen formed lasting relationships with the shoe designers of the time. 'Ferragamos' in the 1950s were every bit as out there as 'Manolos' are today. Just as Sarah Jessica Parker will always be associated with Manolo Blahnik, Marilyn Monroe was known to be devoted fan of Salvatore Ferragamo." (Deeble 33)

"In The Seven Year Itch, when Marilyn stands above the subway grating, her skirt floats up to reveal a pair of peep-toes, spike-heeled Ferragamo slingbacks. Meanwhile Ava Gardner, star of the 1954 film The Barefoot Contessa, adored Roger Vivier's creations for Dior." (Deeble 35)

Hollywood starlets still wear their favorite designer shoes on film, during red carpet events, while traveling and when out and about running errands. Hollywood still associates stilettos with sex in films. Women still want the shoes that their favorite celebrities wear on screen and in fashion magazines. And men still want their women to dress up in and out of the bedroom in stilettos (and some want to wear heels themselves!).

BOUDOIR STILETTOS

It's nice to show off your Jimmy Choos and Manolo Blahniks, but who says you have to go out to a nightclub or fancy restaurant to do it? Stilettos can be just the right touch for some kinky bedroom games. You can slip on a pair of your best (and maybe nothing else) and strut your stuff in your hotel room, bedroom or even your kitchen. Imagine the look on your lover's face when you walk into your living room with a tray of fresh-baked cookies and you're wearing nothing but an apron and black stiletto heels. You can mix up the fantasies however you like. Maybe your high heels can become a code for your lover so they know they're in for a fun night or some punishment (or both?) when they see you in them.

Maybe you're staying in alone tonight? Feel free to slip on a slinky teddy and a pair of sexy boudoir heels to lounge in to make you feel more glamorous. You don't need a lover or a night out on the town as an excuse to wear your favorite pair of heels, as you can wear them to seduce yourself and get you in the mood for some self-pleasuring.

Spike-heeled shoes bring instant glamour to whatever you're wearing and instant sex appeal when you're not wearing anything. They instantly turn you into a sex goddess, dominatrix, showgirl, call girl or movie star. They're a simple, yet elegant way to transform your attitude and sex life. Check out the next few pages to see where you can purchase your next pair of bedroom accessories.

NAUGHTY GIRL'S GUIDE TO LOS ANGELES

LINGERIE SHOE STORES

FAIRE FROU FROU
13017 Ventura Blvd., Studio City
818.783.4970
www.fairefrou.com

Faire Frou Frou means "to show off" in French, and you'll be able to do just that with the shoes and other lovely items here. They don't have a big shoe selection, but the ones they do sell are gorgeous. They offer glamorous marabou pom-pom slippers, along with cute yet sexy high-heeled bunny slippers for bedroom romps or to wear around your house solo.

NAUGHTY SHOPPING

AGENT PROVOCATEUR
7961 Melrose Ave., L.A.
323.653.0229
www.agentprovocateur.com

There's a reason this store lists its shoes on the same webpage as the kinky boudoir accessories like whips and masks. Agent Provocateur likes its shoes to be seen as part of a big kinky package that will wow your lover. The store specializes in mules that add a sexy zip to nightwear, but they're so hot that you really don't need to wear anything but them to get your lover hot and bothered. However, they offer a bigger selection of shoes in the store that you may not find online. Some of the shoes are so gorgeous that you can wear them out on the town.

TRASHY LINGERIE
402 N. La Cienega Blvd., West Hollywood
310.652.4543
www.trashy.com

Trashy Lingerie offers tons of sexy shoes to choose from, along with ones that are specially designed by its amazing staff and produced right there on the premises. You can even find matching shoes to go along with many of the sexy costumes. If you're a size 12 or bigger they offer a special selection just for you. Trashy Lingerie's styles and service are so in demand by Hollywood glitterati that the store is for members only. Don't worry, it's only five dollars to become a member.

FREDERICK'S OF HOLLYWOOD
6751 Hollywood Blvd., Hollywood
323.957.5953
www.fredericks.com

A wide variety and good prices make this a great place to shop for sexy shoes, fetish heels and gorgeous sandals. They take pride in making you look good and have a long-standing reputation in Hollywood and among the stars and naughty girls of L.A. They have a lot of locations in California, so it's easy to find a store if you need a pair of studded knee-high boots or pointy-toed pumps. Or you can always visit their website, as they have more shoes online than in their stores.

HIGH-END SHOE DESIGNERS

JIMMY CHOO
240 North Rodeo Dr., Beverly Hills
310.860.9045
www.jimmychoo.com

I love Jimmy Choo shoes! The colors are beautiful, the styles are elegant and the looks are always sexy and classy. Yes, Jimmy Choo's footwear can be expensive, but once you step inside a pair you'll understand why women must have them. The quality is world-class and when you step out in Jimmy Choo shoes everyone knows you mean business. Just ask for Nikki at the Rodeo Drive location, as she can help you with anything and make your shopping experience pleasurable.

ARTYCE DESIGNS
310.838.7463
www.artycedesigns.com

You can visit their showroom, but it's only by appointment. They let you custom-design your shoes after they've created them, or you can have shoes customized for any occasion. You tell them how you want your shoes to look by choosing the color, shape and even personalized labels inside and underneath the shoes—and then they make them for you. If you love sparkles, then this is the shoe store for you!

CHRISTIAN LOUBOUTIN
7961 Melrose Ave., L.A.
323.653.0229
www.christianlouboutin.com

Christian Louboutin makes high-quality designer shoes that are sought after by beautiful women the world over. You can get "boutique exclusives," "sky-high" pumps or even sharp men's shoes for your lover. Louboutin is a top-notch designer who comes out with new collections twice a year, so you can expect the best. But you do need to keep up with their collections, as they sell out fast. So if you want a pair of their most popular shoes, then good luck.

VINTAGE SHOE STORE

REMIX VINTAGE SHOES
7605 ½ Beverly Blvd., L.A.
888.254.1813
www.remixvintageshoes.com

If you need vintage shoes to go with your vintage 1950s glamour dress, this is the place. The store offers never-worn vintage shoes and authentic reproductions from the 1920s to 1970s. It's like a museum of shoes in there and you can see a lot of their wares at local swing-dance clubs, hot-rod events and rock-a-billy concerts. You can even find amazing, hard-to-find vintage dresses, jackets, jewelry and so much more.

NAUGHTY SHOPPING

DEPARTMENT SHOE STORES

If you're looking for a wide variety of designer shoes and want to take your time choosing between styles and designers, you can make a shopping trip out to Neiman Marcus, Saks Fifth Avenue and Barneys. All three carry a large choice of designer footwear and they're all located next to Rodeo Drive. It'd be a fun day trip with your girlfriends, as they are all right next to each other so you don't have to walk far.

NEIMAN MARCUS
9700 Wilshire Blvd., Beverly Hills
310.550.5900
www.neimanmarcus.com

SAKS FIFTH AVENUE
9600 Wilshire Blvd., Beverly Hills
310.275.4211
www.saksfifthavenue.com

BARNEYS NEW YORK BEVERLY HILLS
9570 Wilshire Blvd., Beverly Hills
310.276.440
www.barneys.com

HISTORY OF DILDOS IN LOS ANGELES

If you wanted to buy a dildo back in the day, you would have to purchase a "personal massager" from a Sears catalog. Dildos have gone from catalogs to seedy truck-stop stores to high-end mainstream boutiques.

In Los Angeles, Pleasure Chest became the original sex-toy shop in 1975 when it opened its first store. During the '70s, it was the first erotic store to create a "boutique" atmosphere. Other adult stores at the time were usually painted yellow on the outside and had all of the windows and doors covered up with brown paper and the words "XXX" and "ADULT" out front, which created a barrier of entry and had a very closed-off feeling for women. However, the Pleasure Chest had department-style display windows, friendly and knowledgeable sales staff and was nicely lit with interesting store displays. They started at the height of the sexual revolution when people were starting to express their sexuality much more openly.

NAUGHTY GIRL'S GUIDE TO LOS ANGELES

The biggest distributor of dildos and vibrators in the world is located in Chino, California. California Exotic Novelties is a company created and ran by women who seek to provide the world's best sex toys. They are the nation's leading manufacturer of adult toys and novelties and have been at the forefront of research and development of sexual products since the early 1990s.

Luckily, we don't have to buy our sex toys at seedy stores anymore (unless you have a fetish for them!). There are now tons of high-end sex-toy stores made to make women feel more comfortable when shopping. Plus, sex toys have come a long way. You can now choose from many different colors, sizes and shapes. You can even get your name engraved on your new play toy. Choices range from a $5 sex toy to a $3,000 24-karat gold vibrator. With so many options, what's a girl to do? I've narrowed them down for you by listing the best sex stores in Los Angeles where you can safely shop for your naughty getaway, frisky evening with your lover or a solo night of pleasure.

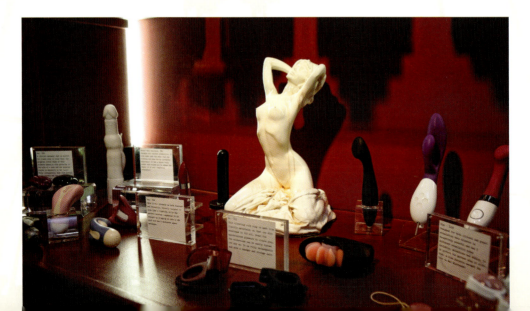

—— NAUGHTY HISTORY ——

SEX TOY STORES

PURE DELISH
10746 Washington Blvd., Culver City
310.591.8792
1929 Lincoln Blvd., Santa Monica
310.452.4520
www.puredelish.com

This cute, colorful store also sells exotic clubwear, footwear and other delights apart from exotic toys. They even have a great selection of costumes for those who want to play dress-up, along with pole-dancing classes. If you're looking for a great gift for yourself or someone special, they offer a "Toy of the Month Club" where you'll receive a naughty toy each month.

A TOUCH OF ROMANCE
5901 S. Sepulveda Blvd., Culver City
310.391.1346
www.atouchofromance.com

They have a special "Ladies Night" that highlights specific products and how to use them for the best effects. They can help you find the perfect sex toy, along with how to use it and get the most pleasure from it. They have a big store in Culver City with lots of naughty goods at reasonable prices. Also, it's a great place for couples to shop, as the staff is very helpful in finding items for the both of you to enjoy.

NAUGHTY GIRL'S GUIDE TO LOS ANGELES

HUSTLER HOLLYWOOD
8920 W. Sunset Blvd., West Hollywood
310.860.9009
www.hustlerhollywood.com

This huge store is the Barnes & Noble of sex toy stores. They offer a big collection of lingerie, sex toys, naughty videos, books and more. And while you're shopping you can relax at their café and catch up on some erotic literature or take a stroll outside to see their "walk of fame" where famous porn stars have left their mark.

NAUGHTY SHOPPING

BONKUM
www.bonkum.com

Their "Bonk'er" restraint device can help you and your lover achieve positions you never thought possible. You have to see it to believe it. So check out their online videos that show you different ways to use it for maximum pleasure. Plus, they sell naughty sex toys, fetish gear, sex furniture by Liberator and much more on their website. Their company is located in L.A., but they sell their Bonk'er products all over the U.S. Check their website for store locations.

THE PLEASURE CHEST
7733 Santa Monica Blvd., West Hollywood
800.753.4536
www.thepleasurechest.com

They became the original sex toy shop in L.A. in 1975 when they opened their first store here, creating the first "boutique" atmosphere. It's a great sex shop that offers free sex classes every month. Plus the staff is very friendly and well-educated on all their products. They can show you how to use the sex toy you just bought from them or help you find the right one for you or your lover.

NAUGHTY GIRL'S GUIDE TO LOS ANGELES

SECRET DESIRES
www.secretd.net

They have three locations (Santa Monica, Culver City and Torrance), so it's easy to stop by one of them and pick up any kind of sex toy or naughty costume you might want for your frisky trip. You'll find plenty of naughty goods in all three of their stores to help you spice up your sex life.

BURLESQUE & PINUP STORES

If you've had a few burlesque lessons and now need a fabulous outfit for your first show, or if you just want to tease your lover with a private dance in a special outfit, you might want to visit the stores and websites on the next few pages. They can help you find or custom-make the perfect burlesque costume that will make you feel sexy and wow your audience—no matter who you perform for.

Or maybe you're looking for that cute pinup outfit for your next photo shoot, costume party or dress-up session for your lover. There are tons of costume shops and lingerie stores in L.A. that sell the perfect pinup outfit for any occasion.

Many of the items you'll find at these stores can be used to spice up a night of fun. For example, you can run your feather boa up and down your lover's body to tease them. You can also play dress-up by being a famous burlesque performer giving your lover a "special audition dance" or a 1940s pinup model or a femme fatale who walks into your lover's "detective's office" to hire him for a special mission.

TRASHY LINGERIE
402 N. La Cienega Blvd., West Hollywood
310.652.4543
www.trashy.com

They have all your costuming needs under one roof: custom outfits, props, shoes, pinup costumes and burlesque-style lingerie. You can be anyone you want when you enter this store. Need to get a costume so you can sell cigarettes and condoms at your burlesque troop's upcoming show? Look no further! Or maybe you want to dress up as a sailor girl and get lucky with some seamen.

BETTIE PAGE CLOTHING
6650 Hollywood Blvd., Hollywood
323.461.4014
www.bettiepageclothing.com

If you want a vintage 1940s or 1950s look for your burlesque costume or night out on the town, this is the place to get it. Their gorgeous pinup dresses have been worn on the red carpet by many famous celebrities. And they're not for just playing dress-up, as you can wear many of these dresses to work or out on a date. They're perfect for any occasion. It's best to visit their store, as they have a lot more options than online. Also, they sell a small selection of lingerie in their store too.

FAIRE FROU FROU

― NAUGHTY SHOPPING ―

FAIRE FROU FROU
13017 Ventura Blvd., Studio City
818.783.4970
www.fairefroufrou.com

When you're done looking at their gorgeous lingerie, be sure to check out their lovely burlesque and pinup accessories. Their ostrich feather boas, bunny slippers and pinup lingerie are to die for. They offer high-end lingerie and accessories for those Dita Von Teese divas who only want the best. The same burlesque performer who designs all of Dita Von Teese's costumes also makes special designs for Faire Frou Frou.

IT'S A CHICK
818.404.9459
www.itsachick.com

Founder and burlesque instructor Penny Starr Jr. has been making costumes and tassels for burlesque dancers for years. She can help you with all your costuming needs by designing you the perfect custom-made outfit. If you just want something simple, you can purchase anyone of her premade items for sale on her website.

NAUGHTY GIRL'S GUIDE TO LOS ANGELES

PINUP GIRL CLOTHING
866.208.7831
www.pinupgirlclothing.com

This great website sells pinup and burlesque lingerie, tassels, swimwear, heels, handbags, jewelry, gloves and clothing that will make you look like you just stepped out of a vintage magazine from the 1950s. They have a huge collection of beautiful dresses to choose from—including day, work and evening dresses. They even sell plus-size dresses and swimwear for those with hourglass curves.

FETISH STORES

L.A.'s fetishes are sex and celebrities. People can't get enough of both here. No matter where you turn there is always some Hollywood celebrity sex scandal—and people are obsessed with wanting to know all the details. It's not surprising that a lot of these sex scandals involve kinky fetishes. When you're a movie star, and the world is at your feet, you often seek wild pleasures to escape from the norm. As a result, there are a lot of fetish events and fetish stores in L.A. to cater to everyone's kinky needs.

If you're going to attend one of the many fetish events in L.A., you need to dress the part. Most, if not all, such events have a strict dress code. You don't want to be left at the door because you're in T-shirt and jeans instead of your fetish attire. Of course, you don't need to attend a fetish event to wear fetish gear. A little one-on-one time with your lover could be all the reason you need to put on that hot latex dress and elbow-length latex gloves with whip in hand. Or, if you're feeling a little frisky, you can always wear that latex dress out on the town by going to a restaurant or nightclub. Fetish wear has gone mainstream and you'll see it everywhere now—from runways, music videos, fashion magazines to red-carpet events. If you're looking for a sexy latex dress that you can wear out on the town, some of the fetish designers in these pages will custom-make the perfect dress for you.

——— NAUGHTY SHOPPING ———

SHOCKING THE HOUSE
310.659.1544
www.shockingthehouse.com

They make luxury ready-to-wear corsets, leather and lace here. Their lace dresses and corsets are gorgeous and would look amazing out on the town. They have designed for almost every celebrity out there, so why not you? They can custom-make you the most amazing corset dresses for a red-carpet event, night out on the town with your girlfriends or lover, or if you just want to look good.

FARTHINGALES L.A. CORSET & SUPPLIES
3306 Pico Blvd., Santa Monica
By Appointment Only
310.392.1787
www.farthingalesla.com

If you have a fetish for corsets then this is the place for you, as they specialize only in corsets. They cannot only help you find the right one for your body, but also teach you how to make a waist cincher and accessorize it by taking one of their classes. Visit their website for tips and tricks on corset-making and check out the owner's book on "The Basics of Corset Building."

TRASHY LINGERIE

SEX AND METAL
310.601.7816
www.sexandmetal.com

They sell tickler-floggers, sensual oils and body jewelry that can be used as delightful treats for you and your slave. Their floggers are pretty enough to display on your mantle or atop your slave's cage. And they're "designed to tickle, tease, titillate, caress and stimulate all of your senses."

LIQUID NYMPH
310.507.0127
www.liquid-nymph.com

Handcrafted fetish jewelry is the specialty of Liquid Nymph, especially their collars, which are little works of art for your neck (or your slave's). They are so beautiful that you can easily wear them out as pieces of jewelry. If you can't find what you want, they will be more than happy to custom-make you a one-of-a-kind collar. Their collars even come with matching cuffs and leashes to attach them together.

TRASHY LINGERIE
402 N. La Cienega Blvd., West Hollywood
310.652.4543
www.trashy.com

Trashy has a sexy, naughty collection of fetish outfits. If you're new to the world of fetish and just want to test it out by wearing a sexy but not an

—— NAUGHTY SHOPPING ——

"all-out fetish" outfit, then check out their Masochist line. This is one hot collection of naughty lingerie that will make any guy go crazy!

HOSS INTERNATIONAL
1030 S. Los Angeles St., 2nd Floor, L.A.
213.744.1364
www.hossinternational.com

Hoss International is known for their sexy corsets and bustiers. Their custom corsets are gorgeous and they'll make sure you're happy with your order and that it's tailored to your specifications. They can pretty much custom-make anything you can dream of. Make sure to visit their website

for sample designs to help you come up with a one-of-a-kind, knockout piece. You'll be sure to wow the crowd every time you wear one out, whether it's for a fetish event, a night out on the town or for your lover.

STOCKROOM
2809 1/2 W. Sunset Blvd., Silver Lake
213.989.0334
www.stockroom.com

Stockroom, which shares a store with Syren, was voted by *Los Angeles Magazine* as L.A.'s "Best Fetish Store." It's a gorgeous store with a huge selection of latex, fetish wear and play toys. They carry both men's and women's clothing, so you can visit with your lover and pick out your fetish outfits for that next fetish event, night out on the town or kinky night in. But make sure to check out their website, as they carry a lot more online.

MR. S. LEATHER AND FETTERS
4232 Melrose Ave., L.A.
323.663.7765
www.mr-s-leather.com

They specialize in men's clothing and sex toys, so you'll find lots of naughty surprises to buy your lover for a kinky night of fun. Or, if you're looking for a fetish outfit for him to match yours for that next fetish event, then you'll find it here. This store caters to men, but you're sure to find a few things here for yourself or for the both of you.

NAUGHTY SHOPPING

SYREN
2809 1/2 W. Sunset Blvd., Silver Lake
213.989.0334
www.syren.com | www.syrencouture.com

They have a wonderful collection of sexy latex clothing that is both fetish and glamorous at the same time. You can dress up and look like a superspy or super villain in one of their tight-fitting latex catsuits. They even sell latex hats, accessories, lingerie, corsets and more—including men's clothing. If you're looking for a one-of-kind latex dress, then they can tailor one to your exact specifications.

665 LEATHER
8722 Santa Monica Blvd., West Hollywood
310.854.7276
www.665leather.com

This is another great fetish store dedicated to men. It specializes in men's fetish wear and sex toys, so take a look if you want something for your man to wear while he's serving you. They even offer a huge collection of sex toys for men, so you're sure to find something naughty for your lover that will get the both of you off.

HILLARY'S VANITY
www.hillarysvanity.com

Hillary specializes in both men's and women's gothic, steampunk, fetish wear and club attire. They have a nice variety of goth fetish items here, including some wild long PVC skirts and PVC tops to match. You'll find some interesting pieces here that will definitely make you stand out at your next fetish event. She even designs matching hats that go along with her outfits.

PUIMOND
323.650.4891
www.puimond.com

Designing some of the most beautiful corsets are their specialty. If you need a corset or a corset dress, this is a great place to find one. They have fetish-themed corsets and even bridal corsets if you want one for your wedding or special bachelorette party. Or, if you're looking for a custom corset, they can make you a one-of-a-kind Swarovski crystal peacock one or anything you can think of.

NAUGHTY TREATS

EXOTIC CAKES
1066 S. Fairfax Ave., Los Angeles
1.888.747.2253
www.exoticcakes.com

Perfect for bachelorette parties, birthdays or even just an intimate night at home with your sweetie, Exotic Cakes makes 3-D cakes in all sorts of naughty shapes. They can make kinky cakes in every shape you can imagine: penis cakes, breast cakes, vagina cakes—you name it. They even ship throughout the U.S. and Canada. The penis cupcakes are fun and make great treats for your naughty girl party.

— NAUGHTY SHOPPING —

JAMAICA'S CAKES
11511 West Pico Blvd., Los Angeles
310.478.1971
www.jamaicascakes.com

Jamaica's is known for elegant, delicious cakes that are works of art. They have a full espresso bar and you can snack on a cookie while you're waiting to pick up your erotic cake. They'll make it as subtle or as naughty as you'd like. You can also be sure it will be delicious, as they make everything from scratch and never freeze their cakes.

KOPP'S BAKERY
1.866.396.8429
www.koppsbakery.com

If you need an erotic cake in a hurry, Kopp's can get it done. They only require one-hour notice, and they work with 2,000 bakeries throughout the U.S. so quick delivery is not a problem. They make naughty cakes for men and women, gay or straight, and even groups. They're also one of the biggest suppliers of pop-out cakes—in case you want to jump out of a cake for your lover.

EROTIC ART

PORN STAR'S ART
www.jamesfxart.com
www.pornstarsart.com

James Spinner is the mastermind behind Porn Star's Art and uses his skills to create castings of your favorite porn-star's naughty bits. You can even hire him to make art pieces of your own body parts! They make erotic art pieces, bowls, business card holders and even Christmas ornaments. He's worked in the Hollywood makeup industry for many years—on everything from *Men in Black* to *How the Grinch Stole Christmas*. His work is top-notch. So why not take home an interesting souvenir that everyone will talk about?

NAUGHTY GIRL'S GUIDE TO LOS ANGELES

TIM OF FINLAND FOUNDATION - LOS ANGELES
EROTIC ART FAIR WEEKEND
www.tomoffinlandfoundation.org

Tom of Finland was a famous gay artist in the 1960s and 1970s famous for his portrayals of buff, tough, heroic men having fun sex with each other. His work is now considered iconic and has influenced a wide range of gay and straight erotic artists. The whole weekend, sponsored by Tom's foundation, is a great time to pick up erotic art for your home gallery or as a fabulous gift for your friend.

THE SINGLE GIRL
www.thesinglegirl.la

You can purchase erotic prints of yours truly. I have pinup, burlesque, vintage, fetish, glamour and much more. I like to offer a wide variety of photo shoots, and even take custom orders! You'll find art work ranging from cheeky pinup to erotic to explicit. You choose how naughty you want your art work!

NAUGHTY SHOPPING

LOS ANGELES FETISH FILM FESTIVAL
www.losangelesfetishfilmfestival.com

In L.A. you can find a film festival for every genre, including fetish films. The festival features many short and naughty erotic films judged by famous erotic photographers, dominants and artists from around the country. The festival is usually in the spring and is kicked off by a great fetish party.

Naughty by Night

SWINGING IN L.A.

Have you ever thought about swinging? Not swing dancing, but "swinging" with other people. Maybe you've wondered what it would be like to have sex with someone while your lover watched. Or about the possibilities one more person in bed could bring, let alone two or three more people. There are many opportunities for swinging in L.A., you just have to know where to look. Swinging has been alive and well here for decades and there are plenty of stories of Hollywood stars enjoying a "swinging good time" at luxurious hotels and private mansions.

Back in the 1950s "wife-swapping" was the common term used for swinging. And by the 1960s swinging grew in popularity in Hollywood and Berkeley. One of the first swing clubs in the country, "The In Crowd," was in Orange County, California. Soon after, cocktail lounges and bars began to cater to swingers. Among the first were the "Topley II" in Los Angeles and "The Swing" in Encino.

However, "Sandstone" was the first swing club to gain national attention. It was founded by John and Barbara Williamson in Topanga Canyon at the west end of the San Fernando Valley. A documentary film, simply entitled *Sandstone*, was filmed there and released in 1975. Sandstone's events were attended by a lot of Hollywood artists, writers and actors. To get the inside scoop, you can still purchase the documentary online today.

"Elysium Fields" was another 1970s swingers club in Topanga Canyon. It was Los Angeles' only clothing-optional club for twenty-five years. Like Sandstone, Elysium Fields offered lectures and seminars on sexuality and personal growth. Elysium Fields closed not long after its founder, Ed Lange, died in the late 1990s. This put an end to nudist facilities in the city of Los Angeles.

Then came along the Southern California–based Lifestyles Organization, which was the first to hold conventions for swingers. Some were held in Los Angeles, and they featured erotic art exhibitions, sexuality seminars and plenty of chances to get naughty with other couples. The Lifestyles Organization coined the term "The Lifestyle," which many prefer to the term "swinger."

Nowadays, most organized swinging caters to couples and single women. Many couples prefer not to go to places open to single men. There are several types of events available in or near Los Angeles, so you're in luck

NAUGHTY BY NIGHT

if you're a single naughty girl or if you're a naughty girl with an equally naughty guy. Party houses and swing clubs are known as "on-premise" events. These parties provide rooms and a fun atmosphere for meeting other couples for sex. There are off-premise events, too, like meet-and-greets where you can socialize with other people who share your interest in sexual adventure. There are also many private parties in L.A., but you have to know the right people to get invited.

The main problem in Los Angeles is that swing clubs are illegal. As a result, swing clubs have to keep a low profile. They also tend to appear and disappear faster than a magician's rabbit. "L.A. Couples" was one of the largest swing clubs in the country. It had an erotic art gallery, a nightclub, a game room, an erotic boutique, two dozen themed rooms (including a dungeon, an *Arabian Nights* sultan's tent, a video play room and a mirror room) and an erotic photo studio in over 20,000 square feet of space! Sadly, it lasted only four years before it was shut down by The Man.

There *are* still swing clubs in Los Angeles, but they're mostly underground and can disappear overnight. To find them, you need to connect with like-minded people online ahead of time. If you don't have the time or desire to do a lot of Internet research, there other options for you, but be prepared to drive because nowadays most of the swing clubs are outside of the Los Angeles city limits. Remember that not all swing clubs are

NAUGHTY GIRL'S GUIDE TO LOS ANGELES

created equal. Even though you may find a lot of swinger websites online, not all of them are high-end—so proceed with caution. On the next page I've listed high-end swinger clubs, but always double-check by emailing or calling them to make sure they're still open.

History provided by Jeff Booth.

WHERE TO SWING

ADVENTUROUS COUPLES
Los Angeles County
www.adventurouscouples.com

Maybe you're feeling a little adventurous and want to try something different in your relationship by experimenting with other like-minded couples? If so, Adventurous Couples, run by Jeff and Kris Booth, offers you sexual opportunities in a safe and supportive environment. When you become a member they will offer different events to help you explore the swinging lifestyle. Such events include meet and greets; group trips to Erotic L.A., Sea Mountain Inn and couple-friendly strip clubs; classes on swinging and much more. Visit their website to learn more and how to register.

FREEDOM ACRES
San Bernardino County
www.clubfa.com

One of the oldest and largest Lifestyle clubs in the country is located about an hour outside of Los Angeles. They get big crowds every Friday and Saturday night, so you won't have trouble meeting people. They consider themselves a "true nightclub" with a dance floor and DJ playing music all night long. If you're not in the mood for dancing, they have pool tables, hot tubs, stripper poles and TVs showing naughty films. They don't sell liquor but they do have two bars, one for beer and wine and the other for mixed drinks. Plus, they have a snack buffet with coffee and soda for those who don't drink alcohol.

SEA MOUNTAIN INN
Malibu & Palm Springs
www.seamountaininn.com

If you're looking for a luxurious adult-only spa resort, then drive to Palm Springs and check out the Sea Mountain Inn. It's a beautiful clothing-optional resort and there is nothing else like it in Southern California. They even have a nudist nightclub! Clothing is optional to the club, but I'm sure by the end of the night and a few drinks later you'll end up fully nude. Or you can visit their Malibu location, which is so exclusive that the address of the resort is kept secret until you've booked a room. Celebrities,

NAUGHTY BY NIGHT

such as Halle Berry, go here to get away from it all due to the spa's strict privacy and security. A lot of open-minded couples visit the spa, so why not go and see how open-minded you are? You might be surprised how a weekend getaway can rekindle your relationship.

NAUGHTY TIP #2
HOW TO SWING

THE DO'S AND DON'TS TO GETTING IT ON WITH OTHERS
By Jeff Booth | Edited By Sienna Sinclaire

Walking into a swing club or house party for the first time can be a nerve-racking experience. For some people, this is the first time they've either had sex with another couple or have been in the same room where others are having sex. You should know that most swing clubs are commercial facilities or private homes, and there is usually a membership fee and a door charge.

There will be areas for socializing and dancing. These rooms are usually separate from the playrooms. Some playrooms can be large, wide-open areas, which are great for orgies or just sitting back with your lover to watch others. A lot of people love being watched; engaging in some voyeurism your first time might be a good icebreaker if you're too nervous to join in. Most swing clubs also have private playrooms for two or four people, if you're worried about losing track of whose hand is whose or want somewhere more private.

Make sure to do your research, by phone and online, before you get to the club. It's a good idea to know the club's rules before you step through the door, as it will save you a lot of time and potential embarrassment.

If you're a single naughty girl, you can probably find all the action you can handle if you're willing. If you come with your lover, there's a very good possibility that you will both get lucky. Swing clubs are full of sexual energy and you might find yourself trying things you never imagined before. Many couples choose just to play with each other while surrounded by all the sexual energy in the place, so don't worry if that's all you're comfortable with your first time. Experienced swingers will respect your limits.

The main thing is to be social and friendly with people you meet there. Don't be afraid to talk to people and chat up anyone who tickles your fancy. It's okay to let others know you're new to swinging. Most experienced swingers will explain some of the club etiquette to you.

The most important thing to remember now is that you have to respect peoples' boundaries and that yours will be respected as well. No means no. You can say no thank you to anyone without giving them an explanation—be it nerves or that you're just not attracted to them. It's a good idea to establish "the ground rules" with another couple before playing with them. This keeps things from getting awkward or limits from being unknowingly crossed. The ground rules are different for everyone, but condom use is expected by all.

If you're a single naughty gal, don't be surprised if someone refers to you as a "unicorn" (since many think swinging single gals are rare). You probably won't be the only unicorn in the place, though, as single swinging women seem to be common in Southern California. Many couples enjoy threesomes with another woman, and girl-girl play is quite common, so you won't have trouble meeting a fun couple to drive you wild.

Good swing clubs provide a safe environment where women can feel comfortable. Most swingers know that you must treat everyone with respect, and those who don't know that are not tolerated. You can explore your boundaries in a swing club knowing that the people there will respect them. Show up with an open mind and be prepared for a night you'll never forget. Who knows, you may enjoy your new "lifestyle" and it may help you to reconnect with your lover in a new way.

PENTHOUSE AT THE HUNTLEY

L.A. AFTER DARK

Hollywood nightlife boomed in the 1920s when films soared in popularity. As a result of people flocking to the cinema, Hollywood filmmakers now found themselves rolling in dough. It was still a young industry then, but smart people in the area quickly figured out that all of these rich and soon-to-be-rich movie stars and moviemakers would want to spend their new fortunes on high class entertainment.

Some of the greatest film palaces were built in the Prohibition era. For the thirteen years when you couldn't get a proper drink Hollywood constructed some of its most elaborate restaurants and dance clubs. You could always find an illegal gin mill, poker game or brothel if you wanted, but most of the Hollywood stars and moguls were seen at the famous Brown Derby or the Musso & Frank Grill. They'd have secret liaisons at the Montmartre Café and dance all night at the Cocoanut Grove. After the country decided that a good stiff drink was okay every now and then, Hollywood began opening up more famous clubs like Café Trocadero, Ciro's and the Mocambo.

Glamour reigned back in the Golden Age of Hollywood. Veronica Lake would not be seen wearing Daisy Duke shorts. Cary Grant wouldn't think of showing up at the Brown Derby in his shirtsleeves. Fashion is still a powerful force in Hollywood, but now showing up to the Oscars in a suit jacket with a T-shirt underneath or in a black cocktail dress with cowgirl boots are considered "bold fashion statements." You can still find plenty of glamour in Hollywood if you know where to look.

L.A.'S SEXIEST RESTAURANTS

L.A. has so many great restaurants, but only a handful made the list for "Sexiest." In order to make this list, there had to be something about each restaurant that made you feel sexy or maybe a little frisky as soon as you walked inside. So if you want to start your naughty night with a sumptuous meal, check out these sexy L.A. eateries handpicked by me.

— NAUGHTY BY NIGHT —

THE BAZAAR BEST FIRST DATE RESTAURANT
At SLS Hotel
465 S. La Cienega Blvd., West Hollywood
310.246.5555
www.thebazaar.com

The Bazaar is where you go when you want to awaken and surprise your taste buds. It's for the adventurous foodie, as they offer presentations and dishes you won't find anywhere else in L.A. Dining at this lively, eccentric restaurant is like going on a delightful visual adventure where you have no idea what surprises await you around the corner.

PENTHOUSE AT THE HUNTLEY

GORDON RAMSAY
At The London Hotel
1020 N. San Vicente Blvd., West Hollywood
310.358.7788
www.thelondonwesthollywood.com

This Michelin Star restaurant is one of the most glamorous on the list, as it exudes old Hollywood opulence and sophistication with the most stunning gold accents. If you've never eaten at one of Ramsay's restaurants then you're missing out on experiencing life, as his restaurants are always the best. They offer à la carte and tasting menu options with seasonal specialties and a chef's prix fixe menu along with signature cocktails.

THE CELLAR
305 North Harbor Blvd., Fullerton
714.525.5682
www.cellardining.com

The Cellar has been open since 1970 and is located in the basement of Fullerton's historic Villa del Sol. The cave-like restaurant with structured arches has four intimate and cozy dining rooms decorated with chandeliers, dim lighting, two inviting fireplaces and soft velvet-backed chairs. It reminds me of Old Europe and you'll feel as if you're dining in a private house of royalty.

NAUGHTY BY NIGHT

THE ROYCE
At The Langham Hotel
1401 South Oak Knoll Ave., Pasadena
626.568.3900
www.pasadena.langhamhotels.com

This stunning all-white restaurant at the historical Langham Hotel in Pasadena will make you feel glamorous as soon as you step inside. It's a great place to dine for a romantic evening with that special someone as it has a very intimate feel to it. The menu changes seasonally and you can choose between the tasting or à la carte menu. If you want the star treatment, dine at the chef's table where you'll get to meet Chef Féau with a champagne toast in the red wine room before dinner and experience a customized menu. The Royce is only open Tuesday to Saturday from 6 p.m. to 9:30 p.m.

KATANA
8439 W. Sunset Blvd., West Hollywood
323.650.8585
www.katanarobata.com/katana

If you're looking for a sexy, lively hot spot where you can sit inside or outside and still be "seen," then this is your place. They offer Japanese tapas-style plates for those, like me, who want to try more than a few items off the menu. Don't come here if you expect your table right away or the quickest service, as this restaurant is very busy with an even busier bar for those waiting for their tables. Do come here with a laid-back, no-worries attitude and you'll enjoy your dining experience better.

WHIST
At Viceroy Hotel
1819 Ocean Ave., Santa Monica
310.260.7500
www.viceroyhotelsandresorts.com/santamonica/

Located in Santa Monica's Viceroy Hotel, Whist's interior is a mix of old-Hollywood glamour with a contemporary, modern twist. It's a gorgeous and sexy restaurant with amazing Mediterranean cuisine. They offer a breakfast, lunch, dinner and dessert menu, so you'll find plenty of delicious dishes here. Plus, they have an amazing outdoor dining patio that turns into a bar scene as the night goes on. It's perfect for lounging, mingling or romancing on a warm summer's night.

CAFÉ LA BOHEME SEXIEST RESTAURANT
8400 Santa Monica Blvd., West Hollywood
323.848.2360
http://boheme.globaldiningca.com

Stepping inside Café La Boheme is like going back in time to a 19th-century Parisian boudoir with its ornate chandeliers and grand red room. This restaurant is one of the sexiest in L.A. and has an amazing Tuscan-style patio with a fireplace and beautiful flower garden for those romantic nights out with your lover. Even better, they offer delicious food with an Asian touch.

NAUGHTY BY NIGHT

PENTHOUSE
1111 2nd St., Santa Monica
310.394.5454
www.thehuntleyhotel.com

Set atop the Huntley Hotel in Santa Monica, the Penthouse is a beautiful restaurant that offers some of the best views of the Pacific Ocean you can have while enjoying a gourmet meal. It's my favorite restaurant because of its all-white décor. Plus they make amazing chocolate martini's. Come for the food, views, crowd or bar.

PENTHOUSE AT THE HUNTLEY

BESO
6350 Hollywood Blvd., Hollywood
323.467.7991
www.besohollywood.com

Eva Longoria is one of the owners of this Hollywood restaurant, bar and club. This place exudes sexuality, starting with its name—which means "kiss" in Spanish. Plus, it's a very popular place for groups of girls looking to mingle, dine, drink and dance. They offer a unique Mexican-style menu with an interesting twist that you won't find anywhere else. After a delicious dinner head upstairs to Kiss Nightclub for an intimate evening of dancing and naughty fun.

VILLA BLANCA
9601 Brighton Way, Beverly Hills
310.859.7600
www.villablancarestaurant.com

This all-white gorgeous restaurant in Beverly Hills will wow you with their amazing décor and their equally stunning menu of Asian, Mediterranean and Italian cuisine. It's the place to see and be seen during lunch and dinner for many celebrities. Created by Lisa Vanderpump of the "Real Housewives of Beverly Hills," it is a sexy, tranquil, romantic restaurant where you can come for a candlelight dinner with your lover.

─── NAUGHTY BY NIGHT ───

GEISHA HOUSE
6633 Hollywood Blvd., Hollywood
323.460.6300
www.dolcegroup.com

It's not quite a geisha house where sex is available for the asking, but it's as close as Hollywood gets. This sushi restaurant makes no bones about flaunting the sexy side of Japanese food and culture. This is a must-see if you've never been, as it's one of Hollywood's hottest restaurants with one of the liveliest bar scenes. It's a gorgeous venue with a red tower in the middle of the restaurant with fireplaces stacked in it. Not only will you be stimulated visually by the décor, but your taste buds will be equally pleased.

GEISHA HOUSE

WILSHIRE RESTAURANT   SEXIEST OUTDOOR PATIO
2454 Wilshire Blvd., Santa Monica
310.586.1707
www.wilshirerestaurant.com

Stop by for happy hour and light appetizers at their sexy, intimate bar that features warm wood interiors and candlelight for a seductive evening. But the main attraction is their absolutely stunning outdoor patio with fire pits, candlelight, shady trees, water ponds and an equally impressive bar. The scenery is spectacular and the food is fantastic as they pride themselves on using organic and local foods whenever possible.

STK
755 N. La Cienega Blvd., West Hollywood
310.659.3535
www.stkhouse.com

This racy restaurant is "not your daddy's steakhouse." It features a bustling bar, ultra sexy restaurant and a glamorous nightclub "Boudoir," but their main attraction is serving tasty meat. It's an all-in-one restaurant, bar and club. Start off your night with a few drinks at the bar before sitting down to enjoy a delicious steak, then head over to Boudoir for a night of champagne-mixed debauchery.

NAUGHTY-THEMED DINNERS

THE DINNER DETECTIVE
6161 W. Centinela Ave., Culver City
866.496.0535
www.thedinnerdetective.com

Voted L.A.'s best dinner show two years running, this hard-boiled comedy detective show serves a four-course meal while you and the rest of the diners help solve a murder mystery. You can even take a dinner cruise at the Long Beach location! You'll be amazed by the actors, as most of the performance is improvised. You can pretend to be a gangster's moll or a femme fatale with your hunky detective lover at the dinner and then continue the mystery, or perhaps an "intensive interrogation," back at your hotel.

MEDIEVAL TIMES
7662 Beach Blvd., Buena Park
866.543.9637
www.medievaltimes.com

This well-known Buena Park eatery has not only exotic food but also jousting shows, swordfights, magic exhibitions, dancers, jesters and more. You can mix it up with lovely barmaids and handsome knights. You also get to eat with your hands there, so it's a fun, sexy way to share food with your lover. Afterward, perhaps your lover can show the prim and proper princess the ways of love from the blacksmith's shop?

PIRATES DINNER ADVENTURE
7600 Beach Blvd., Buena Park
714.690.1838
www.piratesdinneradventure.com

You can see a full-blown pirate adventure show here—complete with gunfire, swordfights, swashbuckling stunts and fun performances by local actors. The facility is impressive, especially when you consider they have a 250,000-gallon indoor lagoon in there! After your meal, you can check out their "Buccaneer Bash," which is a 1970s-styled disco where you can shake your pirate booty for hours. So feel free to play dress-up with your lover by wearing your sexy pirate outfit to the dinner show and bash.

OPAQUE - DINNING IN THE DARK
2020 Wilshire Blvd., Santa Monica
800.710.1270
www.darkdining.com

This hip restaurant at the V Lounge in Santa Monica is just what it says it is. Once you arrive, you choose your menu in an entryway lounge. After that you're blindfolded and guided into a pitch-black dining area to your reserved table. It is a wild, sensual experience. All of your other senses open as your eyes take a well-deserved rest from the overstimulation of our media-blitzed world. Imagine sitting in a dark room with your lover and what might happen as you enjoy a delicious meal in the dark. Reserve early, because they often have to take reservations weeks ahead of time.

NAUGHTY BY NIGHT

L.A.'S SEXIEST BARS

When you step inside a bar that oozes sex appeal your posture changes, your antennae goes up and you know that the night holds many promises. A good sexy bar can bring adventure, intrigue and maybe breakfast in bed if you're lucky.

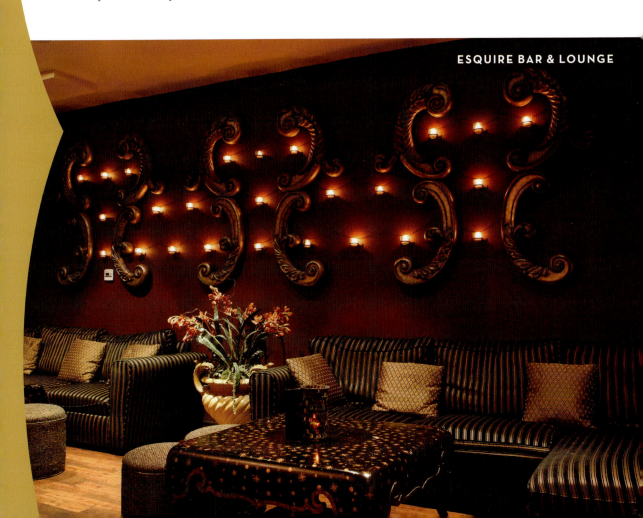

ESQUIRE BAR & LOUNGE

EDISON `SEXIEST ART DECO BAR`
108 W. 2nd St., Downtown L.A.
213.613.0000
www.edisondowntown.com

Built in the remnants of L.A.'s first private power plant, this gorgeous place combines industrial gothic and art nouveau themes. Their food is high-end pub fare and their drink menu is excellent. The waitresses wear sexy 1920s flapper costumes, so feel free to dress the part here for a naughty-themed night. Also, every other Thursday "Big Willie's Burlesque" band plays amazing music as a hot, sexy dancer shimmy and shakes on stage.

ESQUIRE BAR & LOUNGE
3772 E. Foothill Blvd., Pasadena
626.795.0360
www.esquirebar.com

This bar was created as an upscale martini lounge to fill a void in Pasadena. Since their opening they have become the hottest and sexiest bar east of downtown L.A. It's the perfect rendezvous spot for late-night drinks and small talk. Plus, they'll treat you like royalty here as soon as you walk through the doors, so head on over there and get pampered.

NAUGHTY BY NIGHT

CHLOE
1449 2nd St., Santa Monica
310.899.6999
www.barchloe.com

Don't let the big doors intimidate you. The inside of this intimate, neighborhood bar evokes a glamorous, sultry Parisian feel. Plus, they have a lovely menu of French bistro–style food and delicious cocktails where the bartender specializes in creating custom drinks. Come here for great drinks, music and reconnecting with friends.

MAGNOLIA LOUNGE
492 South Lake Ave., Pasadena
626.584.1126
www.magnoliaonlake.com

This was the first speakeasy in Pasadena after the Prohibition was passed in 1926. Back then the only people allowed in were bootleggers and aristocrats who held membership cards, but now anyone can enjoy this hidden treasure. It's now a sexy little bar with a gorgeous patio, crimson walls, candlelight and a place where the liquor never dries up.

THE TAP ROOM
At The Langham Hotel
1401 South Oak Knoll Ave., Pasadena
626.568.3900
www.pasadena.langhamhotels.com

The Tap Room is a nod to the original Langham hotel bar that opened in the 1930s. Now it's a very glamorous bar with chandeliers, a cozy fireplace, intimate seating and an outdoor patio. If you're looking for someplace romantic and sexy then this is a great place to get snug with your lover over fine wines, handmade cocktails or premium beers on tap. On Thursday evenings you can enjoy their jazz band while you hang out with friends or play cards by the fireplace with your lover.

CRESCENT HOTEL
403 N. Crescent Dr., Beverly Hills
310.247.0505
www.crescentbh.com

This gorgeous boutique hotel has a stunning bar, CBH Lounge, that provides a cozy meeting place. It offers candlelight evenings with a warm, glowing fireplace (indoors or outdoors). Plus, you can enjoy seasonal dishes while sipping on market-fresh cocktails or small-production wines. Visit here when you want an intimate night out with friends or loved ones.

NAUGHTY BY NIGHT

THE BORDELLO BAR — SEXIEST BAR
901 East 1st St., Downtown L.A.
213.687.3766
www.bordellobar.com

This sexy, provocative bar, nightclub and restaurant is one of the oldest bars and brothels in Downtown L.A. It features live music, burlesque and cabaret shows—and such luxurious décor that you'll feel like you're in a pre-WWI Parisian brothel. They host some of the best burlesque shows in L.A., so make sure to check their schedule for dates.

BAR NOIR
140 S. Lasky Dr., Beverly Hills
310.281.4000
www.maison140beverlyhills.com

Found at the lovely Maison 140 hotel in Beverly Hills, Bar Noir has an eclectic mix of red, black and white designs, as well as Parisian antiques with a '70s touch by designer Kelly Wearstler. It's a very small, intimate neighborhood bar where you come for the delicious cocktails and good conversation with your friends. And don't miss out on their French Kiss cocktail!

FIGUEROA HOTEL

NAUGHTY GIRL'S GUIDE TO LOS ANGELES

FIGUEROA HOTEL
939 S. Figueroa St., Downtown L.A.
213.627.8971
www.figueroahotel.com

Have you ever fantasized what it would be like to be a naughty girl in 1930s Casablanca? If so, then you need visit here and live out that fantasy. They have several exotic, sexy lounges for enjoying music, having a drink or finding someone frisky. You can choose from Rick's Place, Room Tangier, Club Fes, Nomad Lounge or the Veranda Bar poolside. You can even get a room here if you don't want your naughty Arabian night to end, as the rooms are just as sexy and each one has a different theme.

NAUGHTY BY NIGHT

"Grey Room." You can get as frisky as you want as the shades can be closed for a naughty romp.

ANGEL'S
2460 Wilshire Blvd., Santa Monica
310.828.2115
www.angelssantamonica.com

It might look nondescript from the outside, but this Santa Monica bar has an inviting, nostalgic feel inside. It's a piano bar and supper club with a '30s and '40s setting where you can try vintage drink recipes and sip on absinthe while listening to live nightly bands. They serve all types of food and handmade specialty cocktails—you're sure to find something delicious.

NOBU
903 N. La Cienega Blvd., West Hollywood
310.657.5711
www.noburestaurants.com

This Asian-themed restaurant and bar in West Hollywood is as sexy as their Asian food specialties are delectable. The sexiest area is their bar and lounge, which is a popular hangout spot for locals. There is a special tapas bar menu to make your dining experience more relaxing for those who wish to lounge in the bar area. It's the perfect bar to start your night!

SKYBAR `SEXIEST OUTDOOR BAR`
8440 W. Sunset Blvd., West Hollywood
323.848.6025
www.mondrianhotel.com

Located at the sexy Mondrian Hotel, SkyBar is an outdoor, ivy-covered lounge that offers great views of L.A. and is frequented by Hollywood A-listers. The bar is like an outdoor living room where you can stargaze, lounge, mingle and drink with friends or meet someone frisky. Make sure to get here early, as this hotspot gets busy on weekends and can be hard to get into.

SEXY LA SINGERS

LUCA ELLIS
www.lucaellis.com
www.twitter.com/lucaellis

If you're a Frank Sinatra fan and want to be transported back in time, then listen to Luca Ellis. Luca was the star of the long-running, multiple-award-winning Frank Sinatra tribute show "Hoboken to Hollywood." All you need to do is close your eyes and you'll swear Frank is singing right in front. He's not only an amazing singer, he's also easy on the eyes. So grab your girlfriends and ogle over him while you get giddy over cocktails. You can even hire Luca for private events. Follow him on Facebook or Twitter to keep up with his L.A. performances.

— NAUGHTY BY NIGHT —

MAGNOLIA MEMOIR
www.magnoliamemoir.com
www.facebook.com/magnoliamemoir

This is one of my favorite groups in L.A. Picture four sharp-dressed guys playing sexy jazz (sprinkled with some bossa nova and even a little trip-hop) behind the lovely Mela Lee—a sultry female lead singer (and possibly the reincarnation of Billie Holiday) who can sing torch songs, sensual soul, kiss-off tunes and Broadway-influenced finger-snapping jazz. If you want to hear what a speakeasy may have sounded like in the 1930s, catch one of their many L.A. shows.

NAUGHTY GIRL'S GUIDE TO LOS ANGELES

L.A.'S SEXIEST CLUBS

A good nightclub can give you all the entertainment you need: sexy people, great music and stiff drinks all in one place. Whether the jazz is smooth or the bass is bumpin', a sexy club can be a mischievous beginning or ending to a playful night.

NAUGHTY BY NIGHT

VOYEUR SEXIEST CLUB
7969 Santa Monica Blvd., West Hollywood
323.654.0280
www.voyeur7969.com

This risqué, intimate lounge/nightclub is the only one that has a license for featuring topless dancers. Voyeur caters to a select clientele and offers suggestive design, stimulating artwork and erotic topless dancers for your viewing pleasure. Visiting here is like taking all five of your senses on a sexual journey.

EDEN
1650 Schrader Blvd., Hollywood
323.465.3336
www.edenhollywood.com

The Hollywood haute spot, Eden is one of L.A.'s newest nightclubs and it just opened in 2011. Entering Eden is like walking into an enchanting forest with its amber lighting, walnut wood honeycomb decor, ebony leather booths and starlit outdoor patio oasis complete with trees. The club is small and intimate with only 19 VIP booths, but it's perfect for those who don't like big nightclubs with too many people.

THE ABBEY SEXIEST GIRLFRIENDS NIGHT OUT CLUB
692 N. Robertson Blvd., West Hollywood
310.289.8410
www.abbeyfoodandbar.com

This bar has been voted both the "best gay bar in the world," as well as the "best gay bar to bring a straight friend." They're girl-friendly, so if you're looking for a fun place to dance the night away with your girlfriends without being hit on by men then this is the perfect spot. They even offer eye-candy nightly, where sexy, buff men get up on the bar and dance throughout the night. Some of the dancers may not be into women, but you can still look and fantasize.

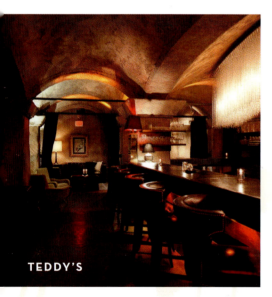

TEDDY'S

TEDDY'S
7000 Hollywood Blvd., Hollywood
323.466.7000
www.thompsonhotels.com

Teddy's is one of the most exclusive and hard-to-get-into clubs in L.A. They have a strict door policy, so unless you know someone or you're getting bottle service don't even bother. However, if you're one of the lucky few to get past the bronze doors then you'll be hobnobbing with Hollywood's elite. Inside is like a dark, intimate den with private caves that can be closed off with curtains. It features glamorous chandeliers, leather seating, candlelight and suggestive photos on the walls.

NAUGHTY BY NIGHT

GREYSTONE MANOR SUPPERCLUB MOST GLAMOROUS CLUB
643 N. La Cienaga Blvd., West Hollywood
310.652.2012

www.greystonemanorla.com

This is one of the most glamorous and decadent clubs to open in Los Angeles in a long time. The great thing about this club is that it's a one-stop-shop where you can make dinner reservations and then stay for the after-party. Dinner service starts at 6 p.m. and the club bumps from 10 p.m. to 2 a.m. If you want any chance of getting inside, make dinner reservations or come early and dressed to impress.

MY HOUSE
7080 Hollywood Blvd., Hollywood
323.960.3300

www.myhousehollywood.com

This club is meant to make you feel as if you've been invited to a friend's house party—a friend with a swanky place. Once inside you'll find a state-of-the-art kitchen that is the main bar, a luxurious living room that turns into the dance floor as the night wears on, a master bedroom that you can reserve for VIP and an outdoor patio where you'll find a fire pit and Jacuzzi. If you decide to take a dip in the hot tub, they have bathrobes for you.

BOULEVARD 3
6523 Sunset Blvd., Hollywood
323.466.2144
www.boulevard3.com

Reminiscent of an English manor with its intimate library, Boulevard 3 has a huge dance floor that looks like an elegant courtyard and one of the sexiest outdoor patios in Los Angeles. It's the perfect nightclub for any occasion and any season as the outdoor patio has a fireplace, cabanas with heat lamps, and a pool. It's the one nightclub in Los Angeles where they treat their VIPs like royalty and offer great bottle service prices.

TRU HOLLYWOOD
1600 Argyle Ave., Hollywood
323.461.1600
www.truhollywood.com

Head over to historic 1600 Argyle and check out this amazing sexy club with hot DJ's. Walk through the glistening grand foyer and you'll feel like you've stepped back in time to a period of Old Hollywood glamour. It's a hot new club that's already building a great reputation as a place to be seen. The décor is beyond sexy and the food there is quite delicious thanks to their award-winning chef.

NAUGHTY BY NIGHT

1 BELOW - CATHOUSE
6231 Selma Ave., Hollywood
323.461.1600
www.truhollywood.com

Located under TruHollywood, this is an elite, private club where you can party unseen by everyone upstairs. If you're looking for hot, exclusive parties and somewhere intimate to make out with your lover, do what you can to get downstairs. The action there will be sexy and decadent. The bar is top notch and the whole place is decorated in luscious reds and sexy artwork. If you get invited down there, don't hesitate as you'll be the envy of everyone upstairs.

KISS NIGHTCLUB
6350 Hollywood Blvd., Hollywood
323.467.7991
www.besohollywood.com

Located inside Beso restaurant, this sexy club makes for a nice nightcap after a good dinner downstairs. It's a small venue, so the sooner you arrive the better chance you have of getting in before they reach capacity. They play great music but have limited seating, so get there early unless you plan on dancing or standing all night.

NAUGHTY GIRL'S GUIDE TO LOS ANGELES

BARDOT

BARDOT
1737 N. Vine St., Hollywood
323.462.1307
www.bardothollywood.com

This used to be Hollywood's famous Spider Club, but has been revamped into a sexy nightclub. It's still a place that loves racy scandals, good drinks and exotic entertainment, but more glamorous than Spider Club. They have a late-night menu for those with the munchies and offer VIP seating throughout the venue. Even better, they're open Monday through Saturday with Sunday nights for private events.

SEXY TIP
Evita Parties
310.400.4690
www.evitaparties.com

I've given you tons of sexy options to choose from, but if you still can't decide which club is best for you along with which venue plays the best music, then contact Evita Parties. They will help you get on the guest list and avoid those long L.A. lines, help you get limo service to and from the club, let you know which clubs fits your style along with the best nights to attend and much more. Visit their website to learn more about going out in L.A. in style.

L.A.'S SEXY NIGHTLIFE

You've come to L.A. to experience a naughty getaway, so check out some of these sexy options on the next few pages to get what you're looking for. There's more to L.A. than just dining out or heading to a bar or club for drinks. For those looking for a salsa nightclub, a mischievous private event, a place to watch sexy dancers or a belly-dancing dinner show, L.A. has plenty to offer.

NAUGHTY PARTIES

SARDO'S
Porn Star Karaoke
259 N. Pass Ave., Burbank
818.846.8126
www.sardosbar.com

Do you love to karaoke or just watch? Why not try a different style of karaoke where porn stars are the entertainment of the night. Stop by Sardo's on Tuesday nights to watch adult industry entertainers get together for karaoke, drinking and as much fooling around as they can get away with in the limits of the law! Some even bring prizes, so you might end up with something naughty.

LUST PARTY
www.lustparty.com

These erotic parties are invitation only, so you need to contact them on their website and send three recent photos in hopes of getting on their guest list. If you do get in, however, you can expect an upscale erotic experience. They hold monthly mansion parties with anywhere from 250 to 400 guests attending. Plus they have special annual holiday events for Halloween, New Year's and others. Penthouse magazine stated that Lust Parties have the "hottest and sexiest" crowds.

NAUGHTY BY NIGHT

SALSA CLUBS

THE MAYAN
1038 S. Hill St., Downtown L.A.
213.746.4287
www.clubmayan.com

This place is a historical landmark but looks like a set from a Tomb Raider movie. On Saturday nights it turns into one of the hottest Latin clubs with a live salsa band. The club is big and fills up quickly with tons of people wanting to salsa their night away. You'll have a blast here dancing all night so make sure to wear comfortable shoes.

THE CONGO ROOM
800 W. Olympic Blvd., Downtown L.A.
213.745.0162
www.congaroom.com

They have salsa dancing on Thursdays and Saturdays and offer free salsa dance lessons on Saturday from 8 p.m. to 9 p.m. before the club opens. This place makes for a great night out. You can come here for dinner and then the venue morphs into a dance club right before your eyes. The restaurant offers tapas-style cuisine with influences from the Caribbean, Mexico, and Central and South America.

MAMA JUANAS
3707 Cahuenga Blvd., Studio City
818.505.8636
www.mamajuanas.com

On their website they state that their club and restaurant is a throwback to the 1940s and '50s Golden Years of Old Latin Hollywood. It's set in a small, fashionable venue where you can take free salsa lessons on Saturdays, dance all night to great music, enjoy tasty Latin food from 12 countries or sip on delectable cocktails of your choice.

―― NAUGHTY BY NIGHT ――

SEXY DANCERS

HARVELLE'S
1432 4th St., Santa Monica
310.395.1676
www.harvelles.com

Opening in 1931, this is the oldest live-music venue on the west side of L.A. They feature the sexy, scantily dressed dancer, Harlow Gold, about once a month along with other burlesque shows every month. Make sure to get tickets in advance, as these shows usually sell out fast. The venue is dark, small and can get very crowded, but it's a great place for Santa Monica locals to enjoy live bands, stiff drinks and sexy performers.

UPPER MANHATTAN RESTAURANT & LOUNGE
3600 Highland Ave., Manhattan Beach
310.545.2091
www.uppermanhattanlounge.com

It's always martini time here. You can watch erotic, Latin cabaret performers shaking it to a live band every Friday and Saturday night. Plus, they have sexy dancers that bump and grind on the stage to burlesque-style performances. Get here early to grab the best seats in the house, so you can enjoy a good dinner, drinks and a naughty show.

EDISON
108 W. 2nd St., Downtown L.A.
213.613.0000
www.edisondowntown.com

This amazing restaurant and lounge has live jazz bands paired with sexy dancers on some nights. Big Willie's Burlesque performs every other Thursday night, where you'll find burlesque-style dancers on stage shimmying to the beats. Visit their website for an updated calendar of events. Also, you can make table reservations online so that you're guaranteed good seating. They have many rooms, so make sure that you're in a room where you can see the stage.

SKINNY'S LOUNGE
4923 Lankershim Blvd., N. Hollywood
818.763.6581

This lounge not only offers yummy food, but offers hot burlesque shows. The Lalas are a troupe that have recently returned from a stint in Las Vegas, so you know their show will be high quality. They also feature the De'Lish Dames who perform a French cabaret-style show and the Dollface Dames, who combine burlesque with comedy and theatre. All shows are reasonably priced, with tickets starting at just ten dollars for the De'Lish Dames and the Dollface Dames and fifteen dollars for the Lalas.

NAUGHTY BY NIGHT

FLAMENCO SHOWS

EL CID
4212 Sunset Blvd., Silver Lake
323.668.0318
www.elcidla.com

Every Thursday through Sunday they have a flamenco dinner-theater show where you can watch traditional flamenco dancing and enjoy a three-course Spanish-fusion dinner. The dinner and show only cost $25 to $36, depending on the night. But make sure to check their website before making plans, as they're sometimes closed for special events, such as Masque Dinner—another sexy dinner show held at El Cid where the fetish industry comes for a night of kinky fun, dinner and fetish burlesque performances. Also, all of the dinner guests come wearing masks and dressed up or in costumes so that no one knows who's being naughty.

BELLY DANCING SHOWS

EL BARON RESTAURANT
8641 W. Washington Blvd., Culver City
310.841.6298
www.raqshirin.com

Shirin, who's a Middle Eastern belly dancer, performs every third Tuesday of the month at El Baron Restaurant in Culver City. So if you happen to be in the area when she's performing make sure to stop by to watch her act and grab a bite to eat or sip on few cocktails. Visit her website and click on the link "Performing" to see her show time schedule at El Baron Restaurant.

MARRAKESH
13003 Ventura Blvd., Studio City
818.788.6354
www.marrakeshdining.com

They pride themselves on authentic Moroccan food, wine and beer, and their belly dancing shows make a great complement to any meal. They offer five fixed-price dinners ranging from $25 to $35, as well as an à la carte menu with reasonable prices. Perfect for those on a budget! This restaurant makes for a great date night, as it gives both of you something to talk about and will put you in the mood with their exotic belly dancers and atmosphere.

NAUGHTY BY NIGHT

BABOUCH
810 S. Gaffey St., San Pedro
310.831.0246
www.babouchrestaurant.com

This exotic restaurant features female and male dancers and you can even join in on the fun by showing off your belly moves. They offer an unforgettable dining experience where you're served authentic Moroccan cuisine in an exquisite tent-like surrounding. Sultry music plays in the background while you enjoy your meal, sip on Moroccan cocktails and watch the exotic dancers shimmy in front of you. They offer specials, so check their website for details. You can even get a tarot card reading here.

DAR MAGHREB
7651 Sunset Blvd., Hollywood
323.876.7651
www.darmaghrebrestaurant.com

This restaurant is in a re-created 15th-century Moroccan palace! They want you to feel welcomed and as if you're at a Moroccan house for dinner. You'll be ushered to your dinner table then your waiter will perform the traditional handwashing ceremony. Afterward, you'll enjoy a Moroccan feast while watching fabulous belly dancers performing.

MOUN OF TUNIS
1521 Vine St., Hollywood
323.466.5400
www.mounoftunisrestaurant.com

The beautiful and exotic belly dancers perform nightly at this excellent restaurant that specializes in Moroccan and Tunisian fare. They even offer private rooms for parties at no additional charge, you just need to make advance reservations.

FETISH CLUBS

MASQUE DINNER
4212 Sunset Blvd., Hollywood
www.whatismasque.com/whatis.html

Masque is a premier fetish dinner show, held at El Cid, that combines exquisite dining with exotic fetish entertainment and the opportunity to socialize with like-minded frisky folks. Everyone must wear a mask to the dinner show in order "to create an air of mystery, intrigue and eroticism." Also, you're encouraged to wear elegant fetish attire, period costumes, black tie, cocktail or anything Eyes Wide Shut. After the show you can attend their after-party, which is held at a fully equipped, private play space where they have many themed rooms to play or watch.

NAUGHTY BY NIGHT

GOOD HURT
6510 Santa Monica Blvd., Hollywood
909.997.8111
www.goodhurt.com

With a name like Club Hurt, you should have a good idea of what to expect. They have fetish events every fourth Friday of each month at Dragonfly. They play everything from goth, industrial to '80s music. So come here if you're looking for a dark, moody (yet sexy and provocative) bar where you can wear your best fetish outfit, socialize with other like-minded people and watch fetish performances. They offer a BDSM ballroom, electro pleasure room and a courtyard of kink, but you'll have to visit to find out what they offer in each room.

PERVERSION
www.evilclubempire.com

Evil Club Empire offers different themed fetish nights at various clubs in Los Angeles. On Mondays they have "Blue Mondays" at Boardners where you can dance to '80s, '90s, goth and industrial music. Thursdays and Fridays are held at The Ruby, but both nights play completely different music. Sundays are at Bordello, where they feature topless go-go dancers for your entertainment. Visit their website for more details, as the dates and venues change from time to time for special events.

BAR SINISTER
1652 N. Cherokee Ave., Hollywood
323.769.7070
www.barsinister.net

Every Saturday night you can find hot DJs, goth and psychobilly bands, sexy dancers and the Purgatory playroom, which is a well-stocked bondage playroom for serious players. If you walk in, be ready to accept your punishment (or dish it out!). Also, you might be surprised to find a few celebrities hanging out here, as they like to get a little kinky just like anyone else.

LA DEAD
www.ladead.com

LA Dead offers different fetish events on various nights. Visit their website to find out more about their parties, as they are constantly updating them. Or join their newsletter to get party invites straight to your email. Their different fetish, goth and industrial nights are Ruin Hollywood, Malediction Society and Wumpskate, which is a roller-skating party. Plus, they offer tons of other events, including charity parties.

— NAUGHTY BY NIGHT —

FETISH NATION
www.clubfetishnation.com

Fetish Nation offers limited, themed fetish events in L.A. If you're interested in attending one of their events, then you'll need to plan in advance. Make sure to check their website (a one-page banner-only site) to find out when and where the party will be held, along with the theme for the night so you can pick out your sexy outfit.

NAUGHTY GIRL'S GUIDE TO LOS ANGELES

FETISH PLAYROOMS

L.A. STAY & PLAY
213.687.8896
www.lastayandplay.com

This fabulous and kinky fetish playroom caters to the true fetishist who's looking to host a private party or have an intimate fun-filled getaway with their slave, master or lover. Even if you're not in the fetish scene, you can still visit here to add variety to your love life. You have to reserve your stay in advance, as the studio is usually booked up—especially during fetish events. They offer tons of different themed rooms for you to play. You can even stay the night or the weekend—or make it a week-long naughty vacation.

––––––– NAUGHTY BY NIGHT –––––––

THE DOMINION
8875 Venice Blvd., Culver City
310.204.6777
www.dominionsm.com

They've been in business since 1980 and provide not only five different playrooms, but a huge choice of Mistresses, submissives and switches for every kind of kinky fetish you can imagine. This is where you come for role-play and creating fantasies. If you're new to the fetish world but want to learn more, then you can sign up for one of their kinky workshops where you can learn to be a dominant or how to spank your lover into submissiveness.

NAUGHTY TIP #3
FETISH PLAY

THINGS TO HAVE ON HAND:

- A safe word. Make sure to have a safe word before beginning any activity. If either of you are not comfortable with a situation, then all you need to do is call out the safe word that will prompt your partner to stop immediately.

- Handcuffs or long silk ties to tie up your lover so you can take proper advantage of them.

- Wooden spoon, paddle, belt or flogger to spank your partner when they have misbehaved.

BONDAGE:

- Use the handcuffs or silk ties to tie up your lover. You can tie your partner lying face up or face down, standing up, sitting on a chair, or on all fours. Use your imagination and make sure they can't get loose!

- Once they're tied up, you can blindfold them. This will heighten their senses since their vision will be gone and they'll have to rely on their remaining ones.

- Caress them all over their body with your hands or a feather tickler, but avoid their private areas. Save that for last, or not at all. It just depends on what type of Mistress you are!

- Another way to add different sensations while your partner is tied up and blindfolded is to use ice cubes or hot wax on your partner.

SPANKING:

- You can spank your partner while they are tied up (or not), bent over furniture, standing up or bent over your lap.

- You can use your hand, hairbrush, wooden spoon, belt or any other household item to spank your lover.

- Blindfolding your partner when spanking them is a great way to tease them. They won't know when it's coming!

- Don't continuously spank your partner in the same area. You don't want them to know where to expect it. Spank one cheek and then move to the next. Wait a few seconds before doing it again so they won't know when the next one is coming. Also, after spanking your partner, immediately rub the spanked area to mix pain with pleasure. This will help to take away the sting and add some sexual pleasure for your lover.

GLAMOUR, CURVES AND TASSELS: A BRIEF HISTORY OF BURLESQUE IN L.A.

Burlesque shows and performers have been a rich part of L.A.'s history for decades. As soon as Hollywood figured out that sex appeal equaled box office receipts, nightclub owners quickly followed by having sexy girls doing erotic things on stage, which equated to more people through the door (and more drinks sold). From then on everyone wanted a piece of the pie, so burlesque-style venues started popping up around L.A. where men could come and watch scantily dressed women perform and tease them live.

Hollywood and downtown L.A. had many famous burlesque venues: the Follies, the Burbank Theater (which became known as the Burbank Follies in the 1950s), the Florentine Gardens (now an under-21 club) and Ciro's (now the Comedy Store). These were probably the biggest locations, but there were many more that came and went as fast as the latest fashion craze.

The Follies Theater was possibly the most famous. Sadly, it passed into obscurity when it was demolished in 1974. Burlesque had gone out of fashion and the Follies had become a low-grade porn theater. In its heyday (especially in the 1930s), it was the hottest spot in town and was often raided (by many eager cops, I'm sure) because the dancers would sometimes conveniently "forget" to put on their nipple pasties and G-strings.

Many famous dancers—such as Lili St. Cyr, Tempest Storm and Betty Rowland—graced Hollywood stages during burlesque's glory days. Lili St. Cyr started her dance career as a chorus line dancer at the Florentine Gardens in Hollywood and also performed at Ciro's and Follies Theater. She quickly became known as the premiere stripper in Hollywood and took stripping to new levels with exotic costumes and amazing stage shows—such as taking a bath on stage. After retiring from the stage, she opened a lingerie store in West Hollywood, "Undie World of Lili St. Cyr," where she created costumes for strippers and sexy outfits for Hollywood housewives. Her catalogs featured photos and drawings of her in each one of her sexy outfits and her famous "Scantie-Panties" were said to be "perfect for street wear, stage or photography."

Tempest Storm, apart from having a name cool enough to be a sexy superhero or superspy, was one of the best-known burlesque performers throughout the 1950s and 1960s. She came to Hollywood when she was just twenty years old and her amazing looks got her a job as a chorus girl.

NAUGHTY BY NIGHT

But it was her voluptuous body and fiery, sexy personality that caught the attention of many men and put her at the top. Soon enough she was stripping in Hollywood venues where she quickly became one of the city's (and the country's) top burlesque performers. She officially retired in 1995 at the age of 67, but still performs and organizes burlesque events from time to time and has a legion of dedicated fans who follow her wherever she performs.

Hollywood couldn't ignore the popularity of burlesque and remembered that age-old piece of wisdom: "Sex sells." Lovely ladies in sexy outfits started appearing in more and more films. Some studios got the bright idea to produce movies centered around the lives of burlesque performers. In 1943, *Lady of Burlesque* was released and many others (such as the 1946's *Hollywood Revels* and 1953's *Striporama*—featuring Bettie Page) followed.

Unfortunately, burlesque eventually drifted away in the mid-'50s thanks to that ever-annoying time killer: television. Once television was widely available, more and more people began spending their nights at home and relying on it to see pretty ladies and funny shows. However, there were a few burlesque performers such as Tempest Storm and Lili St. Cyr who were able to get movie deals and still perform throughout the country into the 1960s. But eventually they both retired and burlesque went away for many decades and was almost forgotten until its revival in the 1990s.

THE REVIVAL OF BURLESQUE IN L.A.

We were blessed in the 1990s when performers and dance groups in L.A. decided that burlesque performances were needed, longed-for and an essential part of not only dance culture but also Americana. "New Burlesque" brought exotic dancing, extravagant costumes and wild entertainment (such as stand-up comics, jazz bands and even professional wrestling) back to the masses. New Burlesque tends to shy away from full nudity or topless shows (that's what strip clubs are for, after all). Some burlesque performers from the glory days of the 1960s and 1970s have become instructors and mentors to the new breed of performers (such as "The Queen of Burlesque" Dita Von Teese and the Michelle Carr's Velvet Hammer troupe).

The Velvet Hammer Burlesque troupe started the current era of neo-burlesque by reviving the traditional American genre. Their girls were all-natural, as they had a strong dislike for plastic surgery and the popular perception of what makes a woman beautiful. All shapes and sizes of girls were dressed in glamorous costumes—this troupe loved bringing women a sense of sexy empowerment. They blended elements from the circus, theatre, Hollywood glamour, strip bars and underground fetish into extravagant shows that will be remembered for years to come.

Scarlett Letter (hostess of the Peepshow Menagerie), Catherine D'Lish, Penny Starr Jr. (hostess of the Victory Variety Hour), and Lili VonSchtupp (hostess of L.A.'s longest running weekly burlesque show: Monday Night Tease!) are just a few of the many other performers who have started their own acts and helped to keep burlesque alive and thriving in L.A. and across the country.

BOOK ON L.A. BURLESQUE HISTORY: *The Velvet Hammer Burlesque* by Michelle Carr

BURLESQUE PERFORMERS

DOLL FACE DAMES
www.thedollfacedames.com

These delicious dames in sexy lingerie perform the first Wednesday of every month at Trip in Santa Monica. They take burlesque to another level by "combing theatre, dance and singing" to give you the best show in town. They've perfected the art of tease, so bring your lover to put you both in the mood. You're sure to fall in love with these girls' performances, so why not hire them for a naughty party of your own? You can also take one-on-one classes, where they will teach you the art of tease and how to turn on your lover while keeping your clothes on.

NAUGHTY BY NIGHT

MISS DAKOTA
310.456.4472
www.burlesquebody.com

Miss Dakota performs monthly at various clubs in L.A., so visit her website for an updated schedule. She even offers classes where you can learn her sexy moves or book her for a party. There are three levels of dance classes you can take from her: "Burlesquetters" for beginners, "Bombshells" for those who want to learn sexy moves and "Showstoppers" for those who want to perform.

HELLS BELLES BURLESQUE
www.hellsbellesburlesque.com

These sexy ladies specialize in parties and private events and they even offer burlesque classes! If you want to check out one of their provocative performances, then visit their website for up-to-date showtimes. Also, they teach weekly burlesque classes along with offering workshops, private lesson and bachelorette parties. You can learn the basics or advance to learning your own routine for the stage or a bedroom performance.

DIZZY VON DAMN
www.dizzyvondamn.com

Dizzy won Miss Viva Las Vegas 2008, which is a big deal in the burlesque world. Visit her website to check out her nine acts that she performs at

Beach. She even won Miss Viva Las Vegas 2008, which is a big thing in the burlesque world. Visit her website to check out her nine acts that she performs at various venues in Los Angeles. She states that her performances "range from weird to wild to wonderful."

THE POUBELLE TWINS
www.deuxfilles.net/poubelles.html

The Poubelle Twins are L.A. performers who are real twin sisters, giving you a double burlesque treat every time. They're also semi-professional wrestlers, but much sexier than WWE as they wear skimpy and sexy clothes into the ring. They call themselves The Twinjas when performing at Lucha VaVoom, which is a wild and sexy venue featuring Mexican masked wrestling, burlesque and comedy acts. These two girls have a lot to offer; if you want to learn more about them and view photos and videos then visit their website. You'll even find Poubelle Twin products such as ties and i-Phone cases.

KITTEN DE VILLE
www.kittendeville.com

Kitten De Ville is a famous burlesque performer and is known as "The Queen of the Shake" and "The Embodiment of Burlesque." She's been featured in tons of magazines, TV shows, films, documentaries and mentioned in many burlesque books. She's even walked the catwalk for

Syren, Agent Provocateur and Jean-Paul Gaultier. You can watch her perform at various clubs around L.A. by visiting her website for showtimes. She offers a six-week "Burlesque for Beginners" workshop, as well as private lessons.

PENNY STARR JR.
818.404.9459
www.itsachick.com

Penny Starr Jr. has been producing the Victory Variety Hour show for four years in L.A. The show is full of sexy, raunchy burlesque, comedy and live music acts. She also has an amazing, informative website where you'll find tons of goodies for those who are interested in learning more about burlesque. Or take the next step to becoming a burlesque performer by signing up for one of her workshops. She's even a costume designer, so you can contact her to make you a one-of-a-kind piece or buy a pre-made outfit on her website.

COURTNEY CRUZ
www.courtneycruz.com

Courtney Cruz produces the Devil's Playground burlesque shows at various spots in L.A. She was voted "Best Burlesque Show" by LA Weekly in 2009. Her shows always have naughty themes—like Comic Book Vixens, Video Game Girls and Tails from the Crypt—so visit her website to see what her next sexy theme will be. She's performed burlesque and vaudeville acts since 2002, has been featured all over the world and has graced tons of magazines. You can even hire her for your next party or event.

BURLESQUE SHOWS

It's hard to list all the burlesque shows in L.A. because they come and go. Some shows last anywhere from one, three, six to twelve months, so always check their websites just to make sure that they're still performing. The four shows listed here have been around in L.A. the longest. But always keep your eye out for new ones, as they are constantly popping up around the area.

—— NAUGHTY BY NIGHT ——

MONDAY NIGHT TEASE
1123 Vine St., Hollywood
323.462.6441
www.mondaynighttease.com

Located at 3 Clubs in Hollywood, this is L.A.'s longest-running weekly burlesque show and is produced by Lili VonSchtupp. The bar opens at 6 p.m., so come early for drinks and to grab a seat as this venue is small and gets very crowded. There are two rooms: one is the main bar where you can just relax before the show and the other has a bar and stage for the show. This is the place where all new burlesque performers get their start, so you're always going to see new talent along with well-known acts.

BURLESQUE BINGO
5025 E. Pacific Coast Hwy., Long Beach
562.496.4287
www.burlesquebingo.com

It's a burlesque bingo game show where the performers take it off and you can win prizes! It's hosted by the lovely Audrey Deluxe and held every Tuesday in Long Beach at Di Piazzas. Or head over to The Mezz Bar downtown, at the Alexandria Hotel, where they hold a special monthly event the last Saturday of every month. You can also host your own Burlesque Bingo at your next party by contacting them for more details. They can customize the game to suit your needs. You'll never think of bingo the same way again!

LUCHA VAVOOM
1038 S. Hill St., Downtown L.A.
213.746.4674
www.luchavavoom.com

Located at The Mayan, Lucha VaVoom is an unforgettable show that has sexy burlesque dancers combined with comedy acts and Mexican-masked wrestlers. It's genius, hot and a blast—there is no other show like it. It's a crazy spectacle where they have nonstop scream-a-thons with wrestlers flipping and flying through the air and performing acrobats. In between the matches, burlesque performers come out on stage to tease the crowd while comedians entertain them with jokes.

BOBBIE BURLESQUE
1253 N. Vine St., Hollywood
323.856.0036
http://www.bobbieburlesquepresents.com

Visit Bobbie Burlesque's website or follow him on Facebook, as he's constantly producing shows here in L.A. He currently has an ongoing show he produces at the M Bar, which is located in Hollywood at a posh, retro-inspired venue. Come here for drinks, gourmet Italian food and naughty entertainment. You won't be disappointed, as Bobbie puts on amazing shows and has some of the best burlesque acts in town. He puts on different shows every month, so check out his website for dates.

L.A. STRIP CLUBS

Strip clubs have been in California since the 1960s, when the famous go-go dancer, Carol Doda, went topless at San Francisco's Condor Club. Here in L.A., the Sunset Strip's Whisky a Go-Go started having topless dancers (not to mention dance cages hanging from the ceiling) in the summer of 1965 for those who wanted a little extra than what they saw at a burlesque show.

Strip clubs haven't changed much since first opening in Los Angeles, as men still visit them to unwind, get a peepshow and maybe a little extra if they're lucky. However, strip clubs can be intimidating for women who have never walked through the doors of one—but they don't have to be if you know the right ones to visit. There are a lot of female-friendly strip clubs in L.A. that cater to women, offering them a safe environment to enjoy the show solo, with girlfriends or with a lover.

Strip clubs shouldn't only be enjoyed by men, as they are perfect to visit after a night on the town with your girlfriends or lover. Plus, they're great to visit to gain sexual confidence and to get your juices flowing. You can visit them with your girlfriends and learn a few moves before heading home to your lover to give him a naughty surprise by showing him what you've learned. Or visit them with your lover for a little striptease show to get you both turned on before heading home to release all your sexual tension. (If you can't wait that long, then head to your car for a quickie.)

Before you head out to your first strip club, you should know about the different types of strip clubs in L.A. so you know what to expect.

BIKINI BARS

Bikini bars are "strip clubs" that have dancers that must wear bikinis at all times while dancing on stage or giving lap dances. However, they are allowed to serve alcohol, which is a plus. Bikini bars can be great for those who have never been to nude strip clubs before and want to check one out without the nudity to get more comfortable, or for those who just want some clean fun. The only thing is that they're not always the best clubs in L.A. and don't have the best quality of girls, unless you know which ones to visit.

TOPLESS BARS

These are exactly what they sound like. The girls can take off their tops and give you an eyeful (sometimes literally if you hold money in your teeth). You can find a lot of hot girls at topless bars, including famous adult movie stars if you go to some of the better ones. Plus they're permitted to serve alcohol, so these types of strip clubs are very popular in L.A. because being able to drink a cocktail and see boobies is always a fun time.

FULLY NUDE BARS

They don't serve alcohol, but as a result they are allowed to stay open later than topless or bikini bars. Watching naked woman dance is always hot (especially when it's a private dance), but be prepared to pay an expensive cover charge and anywhere from $10 to $20 for a glass of water. A lot of the dancers will ask you to buy them a drink when they sit down and talk with you, and that can cost you another $20, so be careful with your money and make sure you're spending it on a girl you like.

If it's your first time in a strip club, find yourself a quiet table a nice distance from the stage so you can see the show and check out all the girls to find one you like. Don't be afraid to tell a dancer "No thanks" if she approaches you and you're just not into her. It's your money, and quite frankly, you should spend it on someone who turns you on. Word will get around if you are a big tipper and the ladies will come to you nonstop.

The better clubs welcome female customers, so don't be timid if you're looking to explore your curiosity. A lot of strippers love dancing for other women (and some prefer it), and a lot of strip clubs have "amateur nights" where you can get onstage and dance for money and prizes. You never know, you might find your secret passion!

There are a lot of strip clubs in L.A. to choose from, but I've discovered the best that are the most women-friendly. So feel free to visit my picks or visit your own.

STRIP CLUBS

THE HOLLYWOOD MEN
6801 Hollywood Blvd., Hollywood
818.845.6636
www.hwmen.com

They offer a "full course buffet" of sexy men! This place was created for women who want to have their own eye candy and fantasize just like men do at strip clubs. It's the only show for women in L.A. and the perfect place to go for a night of naughty fun with your girlfriends and birthday or bachelorette parties. The performers aren't just gorgeous with amazing bodies, but they know how to put on a show and you can mingle with the guys after the show for photos.

BODY SHOP
8250 Sunset, West Hollywood
323.656.1401
www.bodyshophollywood.com

This is the perfect place to go after all the bars close on Sunset for some naughty fun with your girlfriends or boy toy. They've been around since the 1960s and they're the most famous strip club in L.A. They're a fully nude club with two stages where the erotic dancers take it off. Cover is only ten dollars, which is good deal for a fully nude club. But they do have a two-drink minimum, which is common at most L.A. strip clubs.

4 PLAY
2238 Cotner Ave., West L.A.
310.575.0660
www.4playclub.com

4 Play gets my vote for the best strip club in L.A.! This fully nude club is right down the street from Plan B, so you can visit there first for drinks to get warmed up then head to 4 Play for some naughty and unforgettable fun. Plan B closes at 2 a.m., but 4 Play stays open until 4 a.m. on weekends. Also, you're bound to see a celebrity or two here, as this strip club is one of the most popular and upscale in the city. Plus they offer monthly events such as nude karaoke, so visit their website for details.

NAUGHTY BY NIGHT

PLAN B
11637 Pico Blvd., West L.A.
310.312.3633
www.planb-club.com

Plan B is the only non-nude strip club I'd recommend in L.A. It's a fabulous place to visit for those who are shy and want to test strip clubs out in order to get more comfortable before moving on to topless or fully nude ones. It's very female-friendly and great if you just want to have some clean fun. Plus it's a gorgeous, upscale club that offers themed events from Carnival, Brasil, Disco, '80s to Pool Parties.

SKIN GENTLEMEN'S LOUNGE
3388 S. Robertson Blvd., Culver City
310.838.7546
www.skinclubla.com

Skin Gentlemen's Lounge is another fully nude club and was voted the best strip club in L.A. in 2010. They bring in performers from all over the world, including many porn stars, so visit their website for updated events. It's one of the sexiest, fully nude clubs inside with the perfect mood lighting, a warm fireplace, chandelier and private rooms all around you. Their look and feel is a European-style chateau and you can even eat dinner here while enjoying the strip shows.

HALLOWEEN IN L.A.

Halloween is the one day that everyone in L.A. lets their hair down and gets naked, or close enough to it without being arrested. If you're feeling a bit shy or wondering how you might be perceived when you're seen in your skimpy costume for the first time, Halloween night is always a good time to try it out, as no one will bat an eye. To find Halloween costumes for your big night out just visit the lingerie stores in this book, as every store ends up carrying costumes for the month of October.

THE HIGHLANDS PLAYBOY HALLOWEEN LINGERIE AND COSTUME BALL
6801 Hollywood Blvd., Hollywood
323.656.1401
www.thehighlandshollywood.com

The Highlands is a premier club that hosts special events throughout the year, including the annual Playboy Halloween Ball that features the sexiest ladies in the naughtiest costumes. They have some of the hottest

Playboy models at the event, along with a few celebrities. They even have a red carpet where everyone can get their photos taken in their costumes to help you remember the night in case you get a little crazy. They feature seven DJs in six dance areas, so you have plenty of music options to choose from. Plus you'll want to make sure you're wearing the naughtiest costume of the night so that you can win the costume contest and walk away with cash prizes.

KANDY HALLOWEEN AT THE PLAYBOY MANSION
310.499.9581
www.kandyevents.com

Kandy Events not only hosts the annual Halloween party at the Playboy Mansion, but they hold many other sexy events such as Kandyland, Kandy Masquerade and Kandy Kruises. However, Kandy Halloween is one of the hottest and sexiest parties in town, as the Playboy Mansion is transformed into one of the scariest haunted houses along with a dance floor to shake your booty. Plus you get to rub elbows (and more!) with sexy Playboy bunnies, hot celebrities, half-naked women, Hugh Hefner and other kinky people. Visit the Kandy Events website to view an updated schedule. And make sure to visit their different websites to each of their parties, photos and more. If you've ever dreamed of getting into the Playboy Mansion or meeting Hugh Hefner in person, then this is your chance.

NAUGHTY BY NIGHT

THE GHOSTLY EQUESTRIAN BALL
www.bondageball.com

Hollywood Bondage Ball and Bar Sinister present The Ghostly Equestrian Ball. This fetish Halloween party is full of bondage shows, sexy fetish performances, exotic dancers and great music. It's Hollywood's only Halloween fetish event with featured fetish models and their sexy slaves. You must be dressed in fetish gear to gain entry and no cameras are allowed for this event, as it's too kinky.

WEST HOLLYWOOD HALLOWEEN CARNAVAL
Santa Monica Blvd., West Hollywood
www.westhollywoodhalloween.com

This annual free event welcomes half a million people on Halloween night, making it the largest Halloween celebration in the world and California's seventh largest city for one night. It takes place on Santa Monica Boulevard between La Cienega Boulevard and La Peer Drive. The event lasts from 6 p.m. to 11 p.m. The parade starts at 7 p.m., and afterward they feature performers, go-go dancers, musicians and DJs on various stages. Visit their website for photos, a street festival map, parking and shuttle information and what streets to avoid due to closure.

Naughty Business

EROTIC TALK RADIO SHOWS

THE JEFF BOOTH SHOW
www.centersee.org/jbshow/

Jeff Booth interviews porn stars, sexologists and many other people involved in the adult industry. His shows are very interesting and chock-full of good information on different sexual topics. He talks about politics, entertainment, science, the adult industry and just about anything that has to do with sex. You can download or listen to his shows on his website for free and new ones are added every Monday at 7 p.m. PST.

DR. SUSAN BLOCK SHOW
www.drsusanblock.com
www.drsusanblock.tv

Dr. Susan Block has been on the radio for over twenty-seven years now, giving sex advice and featuring all types of people in the adult industry as guests on her show. She offers amazing advice; you can call in to ask her or any of her guests questions. Or, if you're feeling a bit frisky, then you can come to her studios as an audience member and watch her shows live—along with participating in her after-show parties. If you can't make it, then you can listen to past shows on her website or join her members site to watch the video version—along with naughty behind-the-scenes footage.

GINGER LYNN SHOW
www.siriusxm.com/spiceradio

Her show, *The Jerk Box*, airs on Spice Radio on Mondays between 7 p.m. to 11 p.m. PST. Each week she features interesting guests on her show and they answer listeners' calls and talk about different sexual adventures. You can also tune in to the other shows on Spice Radio, such as *Whore Talk*, *Porn Parody Theatre* and *Strippertown*.

PLAYBOY RADIO
www.sirius.com/playboyradio

Every show on Playboy Radio is naughty from beginning to end. Visit their website to learn more, along with how to subscribe to Playboy Radio on Sirius.

- Mondays, at 10 a.m. PST, you can hear the sexy duo of Brandie Moses and Jessica Hall discussing all the naughty things they did over the weekend on their show *The Morning After*.

NAUGHTY BUSINESS

- Mondays, at 3 p.m. PST, Playmate Pilar Lastra (August 2004) and Mansion insider Brian Olea take you inside the Playboy Mansion by letting you know what events are coming up, which Playmates will be appearing around town and what Hugh Hefner is up to on their show *Mansion Mayhem*.

- Tuesdays, at 7 p.m. PST, Playboy Radio includes a show called *Private Calls* that is a call-in program featuring different adult stars every week.

- Tuesdays, at 3 p.m. PST, you can listen to Wicked contract star, Jessica Drake, who features sexy porn stars on her show while they take calls from listeners and discuss sexual topics of the day on her show *In Bed With Jessica Drake*.

- Thursdays, at 10 a.m. PST, you can learn lot of news on the latest in sex research from *Playboy* writer Chip Rowe's famous advice show, *The Playboy Advisor*.

- Fridays, at 7 p.m. PST, sexy redhead Kylie Ireland and Derrick Pierce get together for a ménage à trois with a different "three-way girl" from the adult industry to discuss personal sex stories and to tell inside stories about the adult industry.

- Weekdays, at 7 a.m. PST, hosts Andrea Lowell and Kevin Klein update you on the latest trends featured in *Playboy* magazine along with having Hugh Hefner call in with his "Ask Hef Anything" segment on *The Playboy Radio Morning Show*.

- Weekdays, at 11 a.m. PST, Tiffany Granath brings in many different sex experts to discuss everything under the sun.

- Weekdays, at 4 p.m. PST, don't miss Christy Canyon's signature show for Playboy Radio where she features adult entertainers on her show *Night Calls* and they discuss everything sex and more.

EROTIC NEWS

SINGULAR MAGAZINE
www.singularcity.com

Whether in print or online, *Singular* magazine is one of the best resources for single folks in L.A. You can get everything here—from restaurant reviews to profiles of people who are single just like you. Also, every month they host fun events throughout the city, such as karaoke, wine tastings, bike trips and more. This website is not like a normal dating site; it's all about meeting like-minded people just like you looking to make new friends or join a group where everyone gets together to share similar interests. Plus, it's a great resource for a single girl coming to visit L.A. and looking to meet new people.

LOS ANGELES MAGAZINE
www.lamag.com

This "textbook" of L.A. life can give you the scoop on where to eat, what to do and where to shop. They sometimes feature naughty articles about fetish events, dating in L.A. or which star is involved in the latest sexy scandal. Buy the print version, which offers a different theme each month along with an occasional naughty issue of L.A., or view their online magazine.

TONY BATMAN
www.tonybatman.com

Tony Batman doesn't put on a mask and cape and fight crime, but he does the great public service of finding and posting all the information he can on local adult industry parties, strip clubs and other naughty events. His company, A! Entertainment, hosts and attends a lot of wild parties in the city. He'll share all the dirty details on his site along with photos and videos if he can get them.

AVN
www.avn.com

Adult Video News has updates on what's going on in the adult industry world. If you need to know about big-time adult industry events, where to find the best porn websites or reviews on the newest vibrator, they have it

NAUGHTY BUSINESS

all on one website. Plus you even get to watch behind-the-scenes videos of porn movies in the making, along with other naughty events they attend.

XBIZ
www.xbiz.com

XBiz is the website to visit if you want to know everything that's happening in the adult industry. They not only provide information about numerous film companies and stars, but also free-speech issues and prosecutions in the world of adult entertainment. If you want to find out who the top-ten adult performers are for the month, watch sexy behind-the-scenes videos of your favorite porn stars or adult movies, find out what's going on in Europe with the porn industry or learn about educational topics on the industry, then XBiz is the place to go for all your porno news.

SIENNA SINCLAIRE SOCIAL
www.siennasinclairesocial.com

Named "Best Adult Social Networking Site" for 2011. Sienna Sinclaire Social is your naughty news guide for pinup, glamour, vintage, burlesque, fetish and erotica lovers! This site is for the glamour news of porn, where you'll discover the hottest sex toys on the market, sexy burlesque acts and classes to attend, new lingerie store openings in L.A. and so much more in the glamorous world of erotica. You can even share your own naughty news, post blogs or start groups.

EROTIC PHOTOGRAPHERS

You don't have to be a porn star or nude model to book your own erotic photo shoot. It can be as a present for your lover or yourself. You can give your sweetheart a framed photo of your sexy shoot, put all your photos into a photo album for them or you can turn your photo shoot into a naughty calendar. You can even do a sexy photo shoot just for yourself to celebrate your body, as Kim Cattrall did in HBO's television series *Sex and the City*.

If you're still a bit nervous about posing nude or having explicit photos taken, don't worry as not all shoots have to be that naughty. Instead, you can do a cheeky pinup photo shoot or implied nudity.

EROTIC STUDIO

SIENNA SINCLAIRE STUDIOS
www.thenaughtygirlsguide.com

Not every photographer has their own studio so sometimes you'll have to find your own or they will give your recommendations. I have my own studio available for hire with any of the photographers listed on the next few pages or you can choose your own. I have props, sets and tons of costumes for pinup, burlesque, different fetishes, glamour, outdoor and themed shoots. All you have to do is show up, pick your theme and let me do the rest. I can help book your photographer and makeup artist and you can even get a video made of your shoot.

EROTIC PHOTOGRAPHER

LLOYD ROSEN PHOTOGRAPHY
www.lloydrosenphotography.com

Lloyd photographs for a lot of fashion magazines and is located in Hollywood. He can make you look like a high-fashion sex goddess or turn you and your girlfriends into naughty sex kittens. He also shoots couples in erotic situations, so why not bring your lover with you for something

naughty? Make sure to check out his website for great examples of what he can do for you and feel free to share your ideas with him.

PINUP PHOTOGRAPHERS

DANIELLE BEDICS
www.daniellebedics.com

Danielle has worked with some of the top pinup models in the world, including the famous pinup/fetish model Dita Von Teese, so you know you'll be in good hands with Danielle. Her style is influenced by Olivia De Berardinis and Gil Elvgren and all her photos turn out amazing.

AMA LEA
www.amaleaphoto.com

Ama Lea not only shots great pinup photos, but also loves doing gothic, fetish and horror-themed pinup shoots. So if you want a sexy Halloween photo shoot for your lover, give Ama a call—she'll make you look both cheeky and naughty.

NAUGHTY BUSINESS

FETISH PHOTOGRAPHERS

KEN MARCUS
www.modelmayhem.com/197198
www.kenmarcus.com/studio

Ken Marcus worked for both *Penthouse* and *Playboy* and has photographed thousands of beautiful women, including Jenna Jameson. He's now deeply involved in fetish photography for his fetish website and has been awarded "Best Bondage Photographer of 2010," along with many other awards throughout his career. You can hire him for a naughty fetish shoot or he may choose to shoot you for free, along with giving you all of the photos, if he can put you on his website for his members to see. You can even bring your lover or kinky girlfriend to star in the photo shoot with you!

ALLAN AMATO PHOTOGRAPHY
www.allanamato.com

Allan has worked with many well-known magazines and celebrities, as well as fetish models. He brings a wild, fantastical approach to his portraits that you won't see anywhere else. So if you want something out of the ordinary yet still erotic and sexy, then give Allan a call.

TASLIMUR
www.taslimur.com

Taslimur brings a fantastic element to his photos and delves into surrealist art with his manipulations. Want to look like a sexy Japanese ghost, superhero or something Frankenstein may have created? Taslimur is your photographer for all your strange yet erogenous photo shoots.

HOW TO GET STARTED IN THE ADULT BUSINESS

Do you think you have what it takes to be a porn star? Or are you just interested in how one gets into the adult business? I'm here to tell you that it takes more than a fine behind, pretty face and perky breasts (although they help). It takes a lot of planning, smarts, sweat, self-promotion and hard work—just like any other business. If you think you have what it takes to get started in the world of porn, then read on . . . .

Porn is all the rage right now with Sasha Grey being a regular guest on *Entourage* and having a starring role in Eminem's music video. There has never been a time in mainstream media during which porn has been celebrated more. Mainstream television discusses it on a regular basis. Jenna Jameson has sat on Oprah's couch and Jessica Drake was featured on *The*

Tyra Banks Show. Plus Tiger Woods' and Charlie Sheen's porn-star mistresses have become talk-show guests and Internet sensations.

Everyone, including celebrities, seems to be making sex tapes or posting naked photos of themselves on the Internet. Many C-list musicians and actors have learned that they can give their careers a boost by "accidentally" leaking the sex tape they made one supposedly drunken night. Want to become an overnight sensation? Just put a risqué video of you on an adult website and see what happens. You could become the next late-night talk-show joke or you could become the hottest commodity in porn.

But beware, naughty girl, this business isn't for everyone, as it can be downright treacherous. I've been in the business for over seven years and have seen plenty of people come and go, including those who could've been great stars but couldn't handle the pressure and the temptations that go with the business.

If you think you have what it takes to become a porn star or adult model, and are ready to accept the way some of the general public (including your own family) will think of you, then take my hand and I'll show you the way.

You need to do a lot of soul-searching and research to see if a career in porn is for you, not to mention how to get into the industry. Start with these simple five steps:

NAUGHTY BUSINESS

1. It helps if you live in L.A., as it's the porn capital of the world and where the majority of porn movies are shot. Plus all the major adult companies such as *Playboy*, *Hustler* and *Penthouse*, to name a few, are located here.

2. Read some (or, better yet, all) of the books listed on the next couple of pages by some of the stars who have lived, breathed and worked in the adult industry. Learn how they got into it, along with how they handled it or didn't, to see if you have what it takes. Some people leave the business with no regrets. But for others it haunts them for life, so make sure it's something you can live with. Once you think you're ready, then read the books listed on pages 367-369 on how to get started in the adult business.

3. If you still think you have what it takes, then turn to page 371 to learn more about coaching services to help you get started in the industry. Another good idea is to go behind the scenes on a porn set and get your feet (and maybe something else) wet. You can also take courses on how to make your first adult movie by visiting the adult seminar websites I've listed.

4. Once you've learned a little bit about the industry and you're ready to take the plunge, start by getting some sexy photos taken of yourself. You can find a list of photographers who

specialize in nude and erotic photography on pages 350-354. Once you have some photos you can submit them to the adult modeling agencies on pages 375-377 to help you get work in either nude modeling or adult films.

5. You can also take control of your own business by starting a website and being your own boss. Visit pages 372-373 to find website designers, video and music editors, along with websites where you can look for models to appear with you on your website and more. Remember that this is the harder route to take, so I suggest that you start with an adult modeling agency to get your feet wet and to make sure this is something you really want to do for a living before investing a lot of money.

PORN STARS' BIOGRAPHIES

I've included a list of books to read to learn more about the porn industry and the women who run it. Women have much more power now in this industry than ever before, with more and more women directing quality porn. Without us naughty girls, the industry wouldn't exist—as women are the ones who really hold the power in the adult business. The following books will show you who could and couldn't handle the stresses of the porn business, along with women who are pioneers and changing pornography for the better.

THE SECRET LIVES OF HYAPATIA LEE, BY HYAPATIA LEE

Hyapatia Lee was one of the queens of porn in the 1980s and 1990s, but it wasn't an easy road for her. She goes into her personal life in great detail and talks a lot about the business of porn. She pulls no punches and discusses the ugly sides of the industry without holding back. This book also shows the reader that if you're not wise with your money and don't save, then all of your hard work was in vain. She was left with nothing to show for in the end and left the business with a negative attitude.

LIGHTS, CAMERA, SEX!, BY CHRISTY CANYON

This autobiography is the opposite of Hyapatia Lee's book in that Christy Canyon isn't negative about the adult business. She discusses the toll her career decision took on the relationship with her parents and how hard she worked to get them back in her life. It's a wonderful and interesting read about her start in the porn industry back in 1984 and how she became the world's leading porn star, selling millions of videos. She also tells all about sexy encounters with celebrities and juicy stories about porn stars Traci Lords, Ginger Lynn, Ron Jeremy and Peter North, to name a few.

SINNER TAKES ALL: A MEMOIR OF LOVE AND PORN, BY TERA PATRICK

Tera Patrick's book deals quite a bit with her marriage, how she and her husband, Patrick, built her porn empire and then how her marriage fell apart. It also is frank about Patrick's battles with depression, manic behavior and addictions. Her book is either a cautionary tale or it's a life-affirming account of a woman coming out on top in a competitive and risky business.

TRACI LORDS: UNDERNEATH IT ALL, BY TRACI LORDS

Traci Lords was involved in one of the biggest porn scandals of all time when she used a fake I.D. stating that she was over eighteen years old so that she could star in porn movies and adult magazines. However, she was a minor when she starred in those movies. She became the biggest porn star in the world during the 1980s. The resulting fallout once her ruse was discovered propelled her to even higher stardom and infamy. This book deals a lot with her troubled past, sexual abuse and how porn affected the rest of her life.

ANATOMY OF AN ADULT FILM, BY SUNSET THOMAS AND R. RICHARD

This entertaining, quick read discusses the adult film industry in concise chapters and is an incisive introduction to what it's like to work in the business. There are also some sexy stories about Thomas' work as an escort and insightful details about her start as a topless dancer. There's not much Thomas hasn't done in the adult business, making this book is a great read for anyone interested in getting in it.

NAKED AMBITION: WOMEN WHO ARE CHANGING PORNOGRAPHY, BY CARLY MILNE

This is a collection of essays by and interviews of women who are big movers and shakers in the adult industry, including Tera Patrick, Jenna Jameson and Nina Hartley, to name a few. Each one talks about their careers and how the business has changed during their years in the industry. It's a book about amazing women who are trailblazers in the world of porn. It shows how many women are out there directing porn, opening their own women-friendly sex shops and taking charge of their careers in the adult industry.

THE DEVIL MADE ME DO IT, BY GEORGINA SPELVIN

This fun book is from the woman who became the star of *The Devil in Miss Jones* (and thus one of the biggest porn stars of the 1970s) after she applied to be the film's caterer. It's a great look at the golden age of porn and how far the industry has come since then. It's not a cautionary tale about the industry—she gives no excuses or apologies about her life in porn. And she has no problem sharing juicy details about her romps with celebrities and taking the road less traveled.

ORDEAL, BY LINDA LOVELACE

Linda Lovelace, the star of *Deep Throat*, tells a gut-wrenching tale in this book about her abusive husband, the rough side of the industry and how powerless she felt despite being the star of the most famous porn movie of the 1970s. She gives details of how her husband enslaved her by forcing her into prostitution, along with raping and beating her. If you want to know how rough this business can be if you have low self-esteem and let people take advantage of you, then you should read this book.

NAUGHTY BUSINESS

HOW TO MAKE LOVE LIKE A PORN STAR: A CAUTIONARY TALE, BY JENNA JAMESON

The key word in this title is "cautionary." Jenna Jameson tells all about her low self-confidence, daddy issues, sexual abuse, abusive relationships and her horrific addictions that almost took her life. She talks a little bit about the glamorous side of the business, but also how it kept her from having meaningful relationships and didn't do anything to help curb her addictions. Hard to read at times due to her low self-confidence and how she let men treat her, but an amazing read that you will find hard to put down until you've finished the book.

ADULT INDUSTRY BOOKS

Have you ever thought about getting into the adult industry, but not sure where to start or who to ask? Then check out the books listed here, as they will all help you with getting your foot in the door and more. Not everyone has to be a porno star to make it big or turn it into a business. You can easily be a behind-the-scenes star by starting your own website and hiring girls to appear in your films. There are so many different things that you can do in this industry, so find out, if you're interested, what best suits you.

ADULT VIDEO BUSINESS: HOW YOU CAN FIND ATTRACTIVE WOMEN TO STAR IN YOUR OWN ADULT FILMS, MAKE MONEY, AND QUIT WORK IN 7 WEEKS, BY RAY WEST

Want to know how to find sexy girls to star in your films, how to market your movies overseas and how to begin the construction of your own porn kingdom? This book gives you easy-to-follow advice on how to do it.

ADULT WEBSITE MONEY: HOW TO BUILD, START AND MARKET AN ADULT WEBSITE BUSINESS FOR LITTLE TO NO COST IN 30 DAYS VOLUMES I & II, BY RAY WEST

Ray West returns to tell you what you need to know to start your own adult website, how to promote it and how to make it stand out among all the others out there. Get all three of his books, so that you can learn everything you need to know.

GETTING INTO PORN - THE HANDBOOK, BY MONICA FOSTER
www.gettingintoporn.com

An informative book about a cute gal who started her own adult business on the Internet and used her technology knowledge to create a wildly popular website that led to other successful avenues, such as writing, blogging and more.

HOW TO BE AN INTERNET PORNOGRAPHER, BY LADY SHARLOT

Lady Sharlot tells you how to create a hot website for little money and the best ways to find models and how not to get yourself in legal trouble. She started in the adult industry when there were no books out there on how to get started, so she learned it all by trial and error and is now sharing her advice.

NAUGHTY BUSINESS

HOW TO BREAK INTO THE PORN INDUSTRY, BY CHRISTOPHER GREGORY

Christopher Gregory is a controversial porn director who had to scrap for his place in the business. In this book he tells you how to get it done and what pitfalls to avoid. This book is perfect for those who are interested or just getting into the adult industry, as it will tell you where to start.

ADULT INDUSTRY SERVICES

ADULT BUSINESS SEMINARS
www.AdultBusinessSeminars.com

Their seminars, "Porn 101," will show you how to obtain filming permits, how to start your business, budget, find talent, market and shoot your own live scenes with hot adult actresses. If you can't make it to one of their seminars, then you can purchase their Home Study Course on their website.

ADULT SEMINARS
www.adultseminars.com

They make sure to help you with the business aspect, as well as the fun, movie-making parts. They're big on making sure you're good with federal regulations and will do what they can to help you if you're serious about getting into the business. You can choose one-on-one coaching, seminars or take their home study course.

RISING STAR PR
www.risingstarpr.com

If you're going to get started in the adult industry, then your image matters. That's where Rising Star PR comes in, because they're here to help take you and your business to the next level. They've been in business for almost four years and represent famous clients such as Jenna Haze, Lisa Ann and me.

RT WEB DESIGNS
www.rtwebdesigns.com

They've been in the business of helping models create their websites for over ten years. If you know nothing about website design, but want a nice, streamlined site, they can help you put it together—plus you can manage it all on your own.

ADULT EDITS
www.adultedits.com

You might not have the time, or the know-how, to edit the content for your site. Adult Edits can help and take some of the stress off your plate so that you can focus on what's really important, your business. Adult Edits can make sure your videos are of the highest quality, edited on time and are exactly what you need for your website. This way you'll get the best content out there for your paying customers.

DOUG DEEP
www.dougdeep.com

Need hot music for your videos on your website, or someone to mix the music you've created? Then contact Doug Deep, as he's worked with many models to help them spice up their videos with sexy tunes.

XBIZ
www.xbiz.net

If you're looking to network with other adult industry individuals and businesses, then Xbiz.net is the perfect social hub for meeting new people to learn more about the business. Everyone who is someone in the adult industry has a profile on Xbiz, so if you're serious then this is the place to start when getting into the business. People on here are very helpful and more than willing to answer any of your questions you may have about getting started.

ADULT MODELING

These are all adult modeling websites that can help you get your foot in the door of the adult film industry. Before you contact any of these agencies you need to make sure you have a few good photos of yourself. Once you have some sexy photos, all you have to do is apply to any or all of these agencies and see where it all leads. Many famous porn stars have worked for the following agencies before making a big, ahem, splash in the world of adult films.

WORLD MODELING
www.worldmodeling.com

One of the first and most famous adult modeling agencies in Los Angeles. You cannot only post your photos here, but also list your sex-scene preferences and limitations. If you're only interested in nude modeling that is not a problem, as you get to choose what you're most comfortable doing.

LA DIRECT MODELS
www.ladirectmodels.com

Get your glamour photos ready, because this site is full of the hottest women in L.A. who are looking to work in the industry. Take a look to see how other models chose their posted photos. Like World Modeling, you can also pick and choose what kind of scenes you're willing to try. You can even be available for bachelor parties and they can help you get your website started and promote it.

TYPE 9 MODELS
www.type9models.com

They specialize in models in both L.A. and Miami, so you can find lovely ladies on both coasts for your naughty videos! If you're interested in nude or adult modeling then visit their website, where they have an easy-to-fill-out online submission form. They have high-quality ladies here, so make sure to look your best when you're submitting.

ADULT TALENT MANAGER
www.alisttalent.com

Shy Love, who's also an adult performer and has been featured in over 800 adult films, owns and operates Adult Talent Manager all on her own, so she really knows the business and can help you get started.

NAUGHTY BUSINESS

MODEL MAYHEM
www.modelmayhem.com

Model Mayhem is a well-known modeling site and a great place to set up a profile to show off your work and get work. It's also a place to meet photographers, makeup artists and models for your business. If you don't have the money to invest in a website or just want to see if nude or adult modeling is for you, then this is a great place to start as it's free.

3 WAYS TO TAKE A PIECE OF L.A. HOME WITH YOU

Now that you've wrapped up your naughty vacation to Los Angeles, you may be wondering what you're going to do once you get home. You might already be dreading the daily grind at your job or wondering if getting back into the groove of home life will also get you back in the groove of a boring sex life.

It doesn't need to be so. You can take naughty L.A. home with you and keep your sexy mojo working no matter where you live. I'm not talking about postcards, cheap T-shirts or magnets. I'm talking about naughty ideas and souvenirs you can bring back to wow your lover. You might already have plenty of risqué photos and stories to share, but the following ideas can make your return home even more fun.

- Why not create your own sex tape? You can film it at your favorite hotel back home or in your house. Get an inexpensive camera and permission from your lover (or lovers?) and start filming. You can act out a fantasy by dressing up and doing some fun role play or just get naked and . . . improvise. Make sure to set some rules of what will and won't be taped and figure out who gets the tape once it's finished. If you never want anyone to know about this, then don't give it out to anyone—even your lover. Just because you're together now doesn't mean you will be in the future, so be smart and think ahead or else you may find your "private" video leaked on the Internet by your past lover. To be on the safe side you can always set up a video camera but not turn it on. This way it feels as if you're videotaping and being naughty. Another idea is to videotape it, watch it together and then immediately delete the scene so that no one has a copy.

- Are you thrilled by the idea of others seeing you naked and doing naughty things, but you don't want your grandmother knowing about your kink? Then why not try out the adult entertainment world by hosting your very own webcam shows on various cam show websites. It's surprisingly easy. Just Google "Adult webcam shows" to find sites where you can start making money without anyone ever knowing who you are. Who knows, maybe you'll end up being the next big porn star.

NAUGHTY BUSINESS

- L.A. is home to the largest distributor of dildos and vibrators in the world. So why not bring home a wide variety of toys to tickle your fancy and surprise your lover. If you're worried about your new purchases being pulled out of your bag by airport security, you can always make your own sex toy at home. You can find everything you need at www.makedildo.com. You can choose to make a chocolate-covered dildo, a glow-in-the-dark dildo or a "clone your pussy."

Get your Los Angeles Naughty Travel Girl souvenirs at:
http://www.cafepress.com/thenaughtygirlsstore

ABOUT THE AUTHOR

NAUGHTY LIFESTYLE EXPERT

Sienna Sinclaire moved to Los Angeles in December 2006. She quickly fell in love with the city and its naughty side. She worked for a magazine in London back in 2001, before starting and editing her own magazine in Charleston, South Carolina. Sienna currently resides in Santa Monica, California, where she's a freelance writer, sex coach and adult model, performer and director.

To learn more about Sienna Sinclaire visit her websites:

www.SiennaSinclaire.com

www.TheSingleGirl.la

www.FollowSiennaSinclaire.com

www.NaughtyTravelGirl.com

www.NaughtyLifestyleExpert.com

www.NaughtyLifestyleCoach.com

ABOUT THE PHOTOGRAPHER

Lloyd Rosen is a free-spirited person who is always looking for adventure and is ready to shoot anytime. He has shot editorial projects for print and digital media and worked with some of the most beautiful women in Los Angeles. Sienna met Lloyd in 2008, when she commissioned him to shoot content for her website and other projects. He's very trustworthy and reliable—two of the many reasons she hired him to shoot for her book. If you're interested in hiring Lloyd and would like to learn more about him, please visit his website:

www.lloydrosenphotography.com

BIBLIOGRAPHY

Balazs, Andre. *Hollywood Handbook: Chateau Marmont.* New York: Universe Publishing, 1996.

Baldwin, Michelle. *Burlesque and the New Bump-n-Grind.* Denver: Speck Press, 2004.

Deeble, Sandra. *A Passion For Stilettos.* New York: Ryland Peters & Small, 2006.

Doherty, Thomas. *Pre-Code Hollywood: Sex, Immorality, and Insurrection in American Cinema 1930-34.* New York: Columbia University Press, 1999.

Hundley, Jessica and Jon Alain Guzik. *Horny? Los Angeles: A Sexy, Steamy, Downright Sleazy Handbook to the City.* Illinois: Really Great Books, 2001.

Keesey, Douglas. *Erotic Cinema.* Taschen, 2005.

Lafayette, Maximillien De. *Hollywood Earth Shattering Scandals: The Infamous Villains, Nymphomaniacs and Shady Characters in Motion Pictures.* Createspace, 2009.

Lord, Rosemary. *Hollywood Then And Now.* San Diego: Thunder Bay Press, 2003.

Lovett, Anthony and Matt Maranian. *L.A. Bizarro: The All-New Insider's Guide to the Obscure, the Absurd, and the Perverse in Los Angeles.* San Francisco: Chronicle Books, 2009.

Milne, Carly. *Naked Ambition: Women Who Are Changing Pornography.* New York: Avalon, 2005.

Pedersen, Stephanie. *Bra: A Thousand Years of Style, Support and Seduction.* London: David & Charles, 2004.

Pennington, Jody W. *The History of Sex in American Film.* London: Praeger, 2007.

Williams, Gregory Paul. *The Story of Hollywood: An Illustrated History.* BL Press LLC, 2006.

Zeitz, Joshua. *Flapper: A Madcap Story of Sex, Style, Celebrity, and the Women Who Made America Modern.* New York: Three Rivers Press, 2006.

WEBSITE SOURCES

Wikipedia. *Burlesque*. http://en.wikipedia.org/wiki/Burlesque. 2011

Goldnsilver. *The Velvet Hammer Burlesque*. http://thewrittenwordreviews.wordpress.com/2009/05/02/the-velvet-hammer-burlesque-2/. 2011

Wikipedia. *Cinema of the United States*. http://en.wikipedia.org/wiki/Cinema_of_the_United_States. 2011

Wikipedia. *Motion Picture Production Code*. http://en.wikipedia.org/wiki/Motion_Picture_Production_Code. 2011

Folkart, Burt A. *Mellinger, Founder of Frederick's of Hollywood, Dies*. Los Angeles Times. http://articles.latimes.com/1990-06-04/local/me-389_1_frederick-mellinger. 2011

Our Story. Fredrick's of Hollywood. http://www.fredericks.com/fredericks-history/fredericks-history,default,pg.html. 2011

Wikipedia. *Motion Picture Association of America Film Rating System*. http://en.wikipedia.org/wiki/Motion_Picture_Association_of_America_film_rating_system. 2011

Wikipedia. *Golden Age of Porn*. http://en.wikipedia.org/wiki/Golden_Age_of_Porn. 2011

Wikipedia. *Playboy Mansion*. http://en.wikipedia.org/wiki/Playboy_Mansion. 2011

Wikipedia. *Larry Flynt*. http://en.wikipedia.org/wiki/Larry_Flynt. 2011

Wikipedia. *Larry Flynt Publications*. http://en.wikipedia.org/wiki/LarryFlynt Publications. 2011

History of AIDS up to 1986. Avert. http://www.avert.org/aids-history-86.htm. 2011

Wikipedia. *Heidi Fleiss*. http://en.wikipedia.org/wiki/Heidi_Fleiss. 2011

INDEX

A
Adult Business 371-373
Art 247-249

B
Bars 271-278, 295
    Bar Noir 281
    Chloe 279
    Crescent Hotel 280
    Edison 278
    Esquire Bar & Lounge 278
    Figueroa Hotel 284
    Magnolia Lounge 279
    Nobu 285
    Sardo's 295
    Skybar 286
    The Bordello Bar 281
    The Tap Room 280
    Whiskey Blue 284-285
Beauty 191-194
Belly Dancing Shows 301-304
    Babouch 303
    Dar Maghreb 303
    El Baron Restaurant 302
    Marrakesh 302
    Moun of Tunis 304
Books 41, 43, 56, 319, 362-369
Burlesque 26-27, 33-34, 112, 132, 147-148, 150, 152-153, 172, 175, 200, 202, 229-234, 248, 281, 299-300, 315-326
    Performers 319-324
    Shows 324-326

D
Dance Classes 145-169
    Arial Dance 147 , 168, 173
    Bollywood 169
    Belly dance 147, 154-161, 173, 300-304
    Fire Dance 147, 169, 173-174
    Flamenco 155, 166-167, 300-301
    Hula Dance 164-166
    Lap Dance 146-151, 175, 180
    Pole Dancing 34, 172, 146-151, 172, 175-176
    Salsa 155, 160-164, 297-298
    Striptease 146-151, 172, 174-175
    Tahitian Dance 164-166
    Tango 155, 160, 163, 164, 167-168
Dating 84-85
Dildos 223-224, 381

E

Events 125-133
  Adult Industry Events 130
  Fetish Events 131-133
  Naughty Events 126-129

F

Fetish 43, 89, 123, 125, 131-133, 142-143, 235-242, 248-249, 304-309
Fetish Clubs 304-307
  Bar Sinister 306
  Fetish Nation 307
  Good Hurt 305
  L.A. Dead 306
  Masque Dinner 304
  Perversion 305
Fitness 171-172
Flamenco Shows
  El Cid 301
Fredrick's of Hollywood 25-26, 199

G

Gay 129

H

Halloween 335-337
History
  Books 41-43, 319
  Movies 45-47
  of Burlesque 315-319
  of Lingerie 197-199
  of Los Angeles 17-38
  of Nightlife 265-266
  of Stilettos 211-213
  of Strip Clubs 327
  of Swinging 253-25
Hotels 65-83, 101
  Avalon Hotel 82
  Beverly Wilshire 71-72
  Channel Road Inn 75
  Chateau Marmont 24-25, 76, 82-83, 107
  Hotel BelAir 73-74
  Hollywood Roosevelt 72
  L.A. Sky Boutique Hotel 73
  L.A. Stay & Play 77-78
  Maison 140, 68
  Mondrian Hotel 68
  The Huntley Hotel 71
  The Malibu Inn 75-76
  Viceroy 67
  W Hotel 69
Hugh Hefner 17, 31-32, 47, 120, 336

J

Jazz Age 18-19

L

Larry Flynt 17, 32, 47, 105

INDEX

M

Madam 34-35, 45, 117
Magazines 31-32, 35, 345-346
Mann Act 51
Marilyn Monroe 23, 64, 107, 119, 191, 197-198, 211-212
MPAA 27-29
Modeling 375-377
Motels 89-97
    Coral Sands Hotel 91
    Saharan Motor Hotel 91
    Sea Shore Motel 91
    Snooty Fox Motor Inn 91
    Vibe Motel 91
Movies 22, 45-47, 49-51, 198, 212, 317

N

Naughty Tips 95-97, 261-263, 311-313
Nightclubs 288-294
    Bardot 294
    Below 1 293
    Boulevard 3 292
    Eden 289
    Greystone Manor Supperclub 291
    Kiss Nightclub 293
    My House 291
    Teddy's 290
    The Abbey 289-290
    Tru Hollywood 292
    Voyeur 289
Nude Beaches 183-187

P

Packing 57
Parties 173-181
Photographers 349-354, 384
Pinup 199, 202, 229-234, 248
Porn 17, 28-29, 31-33, 35, 38, 41-43, 45-46, 108, 113, 115, 122, 125-126, 130, 355, 362, 367-369
Porn Stars 29, 31, 35-37, 42, 46-47, 108, 110-111, 115, 125, 126, 130, 247, 295, 341-344, 361-365, 375

R

Radio Shows 341-344
Restaurants 266-276
    Beso 272
    Café La Boheme 271
    Geisha House 273
    Gordan Ramsay 268
    Katana 269
    Medieval Times 275
    Opaque – Dining in the Dark 276
    Penthouse 270
    Pirates Dinner Adventure 276
    STK 274
    The Bazaar 267
    The Cellar 268
    The Dinner Detective 275
    The Royce 269
    Villa Blanca 272
    Whist 270
    Wilshire Restaurant 274
Rise of Hollywood 18

Wilshire Restaurant 274
Rise of Hollywood 18

S

Salsa Clubs 297-298
   Mama Juanas 298
   The Congo Room 297
   The Mayan 297
Sex Classes 135-143
   Fetish Classes 142-143
   Naughty Classes 136-141
Sex in Cinema 20
Sexy Dance Clubs 299-300
   Edison 300
   Harvelle's 299
   Upper Manhattan Restaurant & Lounge 299
Sienna Sinclaire 12, 48, 85, 94, 131, 133, 139-140, 143-144, 170, 182, 190, 192, 248, 298, 301, 312, 320, 331, 347, 350-351, 353, 371, 358-359, 383
Singers 286-287
Spray Tan 194
Starlets 19, 22-24, 26, 107, 197, 199, 212
Stores 58-64, 136, 142, 381
   Burlesque/Pinup Stores 230-234
   Fetish Stores 237-242
   Lingerie Stores 200-209
   Naughty Treats 243, 245
   Sex Toy Stores 225-228
   Shoe Stores 214-221
Strip Clubs 34, 327-333
Swingers 253-259

T

Theatres 31-33, 113, 115, 199, 315
Tours 101-123

W

Will Hays Code 19-22, 23, 24, 27-29, 42, 46, 199

PHOTO CREDITS

All photos in the book were taken by Llyod Rosen Photography except for the following:

Photos courtesy of:
- Angel's Photos By: Holly Port 284, 287
- Bardot Photos By: Damian Tsutsumida 294
- Belly Twins Photo By: Ed Freeman 156
- BeSpun 148
- Esquire Bar & Lounge 277
- Figuero Hotel 282-283
- Fire Groove 169, 178-179
- Geisha House 273
- Huntley Hotel Photos By: Jonathan Rouse Photography 70, 264, 267, 271
- Penny Starr, Jr 153, 323, 348
- Princess Farhana 155
- Teddy's 290
- Trashy Lingerie 231, 237, 334
- W Hotel Westwood 69

SPECIAL THANKS
to the following people for making this book possible:

Adrian Beuthin
Alan Hebel
Alec Hsu
Angel's
Bardot
Belly Twins
BeSpun
Coco De Mer
David Barry
Esquire Bar & Lounge
Jeff Booth
Faire Frou Frou
Figuero Hotel
Fire Groove
Geisha House
Huntley Hotel
L.A. Stay & Play
Liza Dodson
Llyod Rosen
Nik Havert
Penny Starr, Jr.
Pink Lili
Princess Farhana
Teddy's
Trashy Lingerie
W Hotel Westwood